Dirt Late Model Chassis Technology

By Joe Garrison
and Steve Smith

ISBN 0-936834-98-6

Published By

STEVE SMITH AUTOSPORTS® PUBLICATIONS

P.O. Box 11631 / Santa Ana, CA 92711 / (714) 639-7681
www.SteveSmithAutosports.com

Printed and bound in the United States of America

Table of Contents

1. Race Car Design 5
Design For Ease of Maintenance 5
Choosing Component Location 6
Designing For Structural Strength 7
Designing For Weight..8
Establishing Roll Centers 8
Front Spindle Design 9
Establishing Camber Gain Curves 10
Designing The Bump Steer...................................10
Building In Crash Zones 10
Cockpit Safety Design 11
Design Is The Key Element To Being Competitive 11

2. Race Car Construction..............................12
Chassis Building Materials 12
Welding Methods 13
Welding The Chassis Together.............................13
Gussets & Bracing 14
Chassis Reference Points 14
Fuel Cell Mounting 15
Rod End Bearings 16

3. Front Suspension & Steering 17
Designing A Front Suspension 17
Component Choice...17
Choosing A Spindle – Design Criteria....................18
Spindle Materials 20
Ball Joints 20
Steering Rod Ends 21
Right Front Spring Rate 21
Bump Steer..21
Rack And Pinion Systems 22

4. Rear Suspension Systems.........................24
Four Link Suspension..24
4-link Dynamic Movement – Left Side 26
4-link Dynamic Movement – Right Side 27
Chassis Adjustment with 4-Bar Angles 28
Left Upper Bar 28
Left Lower Bar 28
Right Upper Bar 28
Right Lower Bar 29
Using A Longer Left Rear Lower Link 30
Left Side Limiter Chain 30
Left Rear Spring Rate 30
Right Rear Double Spring Setup 31
Left Rear Clamp Bracket 32
Brake Caliper Mounting 32

Swing Arm Suspension 33
Torque Arms 34
Torque Arm Length 34
Braking Torque Absorption 34
Torque Arm Bracing 35
Panhard Bars 36
Panhard Bar Angle 37
Panhard Bar Length 38
Straight Panhard Bar 38
Axle Dampers 39
Setting The Pinion Angle 39
Differential Types 39
Proper Gearing..40

5. Dirt Late Model Handling Dynamics 83
Getting the Car Up On the Bars 83
Rear Roll Steer 84
4-Link Adjustment At Corner Entry 84
Right Side Traction 85
Forward Traction Under Throttle Application 86
Left Side Chassis Lift Limitation 87
Adjusting Rear Lift To Track Conditions 87

6. Shock Absorbers 47
Twin Tube, Low Gas Pressure Shocks 47
Monotube High Gas Pressure Shocks 48
Monotube Gas Pressure Guidelines 49
Left Rear Monotube Gas Pressure.........................49
Left Front Monotube Gas Pressure 49
Damping Stiffness Codes 50
Split Valving Shocks 50
Tie Down Shocks 50
Easy Up Shocks 51
How Shocks Influence Handling............................51
Adjustable Rate Double Tube Shocks 52
Matching Shocks to Track Conditions 53
High Speed/High Banked Track Setup 54
Chassis Adjustment with Shocks – Loose At Corner Entry 54
Dummy Shock 54
Shock Dyno Testing 54

7. Tires & Wheels 57
Tire Selection 57
Tire Compound Choice...57
Tire Tread Patterns...58
Tire Grooving & Siping 58
Tire Compound Hardness Comparison 58
Goodyear vs Hoosier 58

Different Types of Grooves & Sipes 59
Other Grooving Tips 60
Proper Angles for Grooving 61
Front Tire Grooving Tips...................................61
Tire Break-In..61
Tire Pressure 61
Reading Tire Surfaces 62
Tire Stagger 63
Wheels 63
Aluminum Wheels 63
Wheel Trueness 64
Wheel Offsets 64
Valve Stems 65
Bead Locks 65
Wheel Maintenance 65

8. Chassis Setup & Alignment 67
Checking For Chassis Binds 67
Squaring The Rear End 67
Chassis Set-Up In The Shop 68
Setting The Ride Height 68
Setting The Corner Weights 69
Ballast Placement...70
Setting Up For The End Of The Race.................71
Front End Alignment......................................72
Caster..72
Setting The Caster 72
GRT's No Sweep Caster/Camber Gauge.............73
Camber...73
Setting The Toe-Out 73
Starting Specs 74
Chassis Setup & Adjustments 74

9. Track Setups 76
Baseline Setup 76
Banked and/or High Speed Tracks..................77
Extremely Slick or Slow Track, Semi-Smooth To
Smooth Tracks 79
Very Tacky, High Traction Tracks 80

10. Track Tuning & Adjustment 82
Chassis Tuning Elements................................82
Left Rear Shock Placement 82
Left Side Weight Percentage 83
Left Rear Bite 83
Rear Weight Percentage 83
Rear Upper Link Adjustment...........................84
Tire Stagger 84
Brake Bias 85
Chassis Tuning With Ballast Placement.............85
Tuning With the Panhard Bar 86
Tuning With Wheel Offset/Wheel Spacers 87
Tuning With Shock Absorbers 87

Tuning With Split Valving Shocks 88
Chassis Tuning With Gear Ratio 89
Different Types Of Track Conditions.................89
Wet Track Condition 90
The Tacky Track 91
Dry Track Conditions 93
Adjustments for Common Handling Problems 93
Hiking Up the Left Front Corner 94
Loose at Corner Entry 94
Pushing At Corner Entry/Mid Corner 95
Pushing At Corner Entry.................................96
Chassis Adjustment – Wet, Heavy Track 96
Chassis Adjustment With Shocks – Slick Smooth Track ..96
High Speed/High Banked Track Adjustment............96
Chassis Adjustment – Tight At Entry Under Braking............97
Chassis Adjustment – Rubbered Down Track 97
Chassis Sorting Philosophy 97
Chassis Adjustment Quick
Reference..98
Tuning With Shocks 99

11. Suppliers Directory 100

Thanks

A very special thanks goes to all of the GRT employees and to my family. Also, I would like to offer a very special thank you to Scott Keyser of Integra Shocks, all of the GRT drivers and crews, and all GRT dealers and suppliers for their continued support.

Joe Garrison, Jr.

Introduction

In 1995, I wrote my first book for Steve Smith Autosports that gave a basic understanding of dirt late model chassis setups, design, and construction. Now, with ten years gone by, it is time to update and explain all of the changes that have occurred in Dirt Late Model racing. Hopefully this book will provide a better understanding of the innovations and technology that have advanced Dirt Late Model racing. GRT has built more than 3,000 cars and has stayed on the leading edge of late model design, with racing records across the nation to back up GRT's commitment to excellence.

The following is a list of GRT's major accomplishments in the past 20 years:

13 time MLRA manufacturer champion
3 time Dirt Track World Champion
2 time UMP manufacturer champion
5 time Show-Me 100 champion
3 time Topless 100 champion
4 time Xtreme DirtCar Series manufacturer champion
3 time Shootout champion
5 time Southern All-Stars manufacturer champion
2 time Northern All-Stars manufacturer champion
4 time MARS Series manufacturer champion
2 time Masters champion
Eldora Dream champion

Disclaimer Notice

Every attempt has been made to present the information contained in this book in a true, accurate and complete form. The information was prepared with the best information that could be obtained. However, auto racing is a dangerous undertaking and no responsibility can be taken by any persons associated with this book, the authors, the publisher, the parent corporation, or any person or persons associated therewith, for injury sustained as a result of or in spite of following the suggestions or procedures offered herein. All recommendations are made without any guarantee on the part of the author or the publisher, and any information utilized by the reader is done so strictly at the reader's own risk. Because the use of information contained in this book is beyond the control of the authors or publisher, liability for use is expressly disclaimed.

We recognize that some words, model names and designations mentioned herein are the property of the trademark holder. We use them for identification purposes. This is not an official publication.

Chapter

1

<u>Race Car Design</u>

When designing a race car, you have to consider the type of racing you are going to be doing, the speeds you will be running, and the most common track sizes. You must also consider the weight rules for the type of racing you will be doing, never letting safety out of the picture. Other considerations are ease of maintenance, structural strength, basic suspension design, and safety.

Design For Ease of Maintenance

A major consideration of race car design is making the car easier to work on during maintenance or general repair. For instance, all of our cars come standard with bolt-on body braces, interior mounts, nose bracing and deck bracing for ease of maintenance. What this does is make repairs at a race track or in the shop much simpler and faster. Whenever you don't have to get the torch, welder, and Porta Power out, things can be done much more efficiently. Also, we make our body bracing and supports out of 1" spring steel strap so that when impacts are taken, the strap absorbs the blow. It is very forgiving and pops right back into shape. Also, the bolt-on application of any component that possibly might be in a crash zone simplifies repairs.

Other ways of making working on a car easier are using Dzus fas-teners on as many panels as possible. This includes removable fenders for easy access to the engine bay, removable dash panel for easy gauge and brake pedal maintenance, and removable dry sump tank panel for ease of changing oil or checking the in-line oil filter. Some cars even have the whole body side removable for easy changes or repairs.

The cage and chassis should be designed for ease of maintenance for all components. Things like engine removal, spring and shock removal, and trailing arm mount access should be carefully considered.

There are several design considerations that go into a race car that

 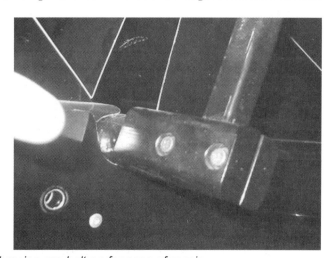

All body braces, interior mounts, nose bracing and deck bracing are bolt-on for ease of repair.

Spring steel is used to brace body panels. It is collapsible but yet returns to its original form after an impact.

(Left) This is what happens when aluminum braces are used.

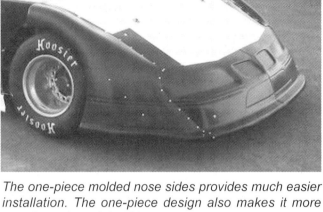

The one-piece molded nose sides provides much easier installation. The one-piece design also makes it more aerodynamic and durable.

The movable battery box is excellent for adjusting weight transfer or weight percentages. The battery is dead weight that can easily be used for handling advantages as long as it is movable.

The Oval Craft dry sump tank is designed for aerodynamics as well as the adjustability to raise it up or down for handling.

GRT builds for easy maintenance and repair simply because these factors also improve a race team's chances of getting back on the track after repairs or changes as soon as possible. You don't need to miss a race or a hot lap just because of a minor problem that could have been easy to fix with just a little bit of design consideration for making a car easier to work on.

Choosing Component Location

When designing the chassis many things have to be considered. For instance you must incor-

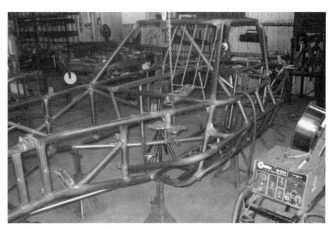

The chassis has to be strong and light, but never sacrifice weight for safety and durability. Triangulation adds strength to the chassis by spreading the loads which are input to the chassis evenly throughout the structure.

This well-engineered Oval Craft rear end filler serves three purposes: filler for rear end grease, rear end vent, and fuel cell vent.

porate the bracketry and mounting locations of all your suspension and bolt-on components around the structural design of the car. Sometimes putting your brackets and mounts where they belong is a problem because of the location of the roll cage tubing or bracing that is located there for optimal strength. In this case you possibly might increase the wall thickness or outside diameter of the tubing and change the location to accommodate the bracket and still retain the same chassis stiffness.

One general rule for component placement is that you want to use each and every piece you install in a chassis to the best advantage possible. For instance, most items placed in the chassis are put there to take advantage of the weight. When putting weight in a chassis you try to make use of it as much as possible. These component choices include the battery, dry sump tank, and fuel cell (it has to be at the rear but can be moved

up and down or left and right).

Well-planned component placement can also help one piece to serve dual purposes. For instance, placement of a motor plate or torque plate serves two purposes — to hold the engine in location and to strengthen the chassis.

Component placement in a chassis has to be fairly practical and is determined by taking advantage of weight and the size and function of the component.

Designing For Structural Strength

When bracing a chassis for optimal strength, triangulation must be used, and the more triangulation you have, the stronger your chassis is. You want your chassis to be strong and light, but never sacrifice weight for safety and durability. You can't win races if your car is not durable, and a lightweight car can get you hurt.

The basic principle of triangulation is to spread the loads which are input to the chassis evenly throughout the entire structure.

This is done to place the loads in the tubes in compression rather than in bending, which utilizes the strongest aspect of round tubing.

A major design consideration for structural strength is the wall thickness and the outside diameter of the tubing used. Increasing the O.D. of the tubing makes the point of failure much higher than just increasing the wall thickness. For instance, if you do a mathematical analysis of a 4-foot long piece of 1.75″ O.D., .095″ wall tube versus a 6″ O.D., .065″ wall tube of the same length, you will find that the larger diameter tube with a thinner wall thickness is actually two times stronger in both critical bending stress and deflection strength. And, the larger diameter tube weighs only 2.45 times more. This is an extreme example, but it demonstrates how an increase in diameter increases a tube's strength in all directions (compression, torsional and bending).

As a practical example, a 4-foot length of 1.75″ O.D., .095″ wall

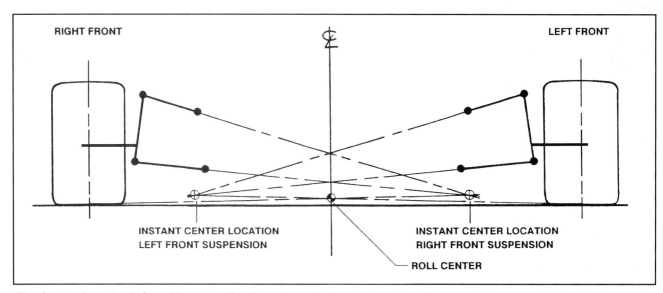

RIGHT FRONT   LEFT FRONT

INSTANT CENTER LOCATION
LEFT FRONT SUSPENSION

INSTANT CENTER LOCATION
RIGHT FRONT SUSPENSION

ROLL CENTER

The front roll center is found by extending lines through the pivot points of the control arms on both sides to a common intersection point, called the instant center. Then a line is projected from the instant center back to the center of the tire. The true roll center is where the instant center swing arms of the left front and the right front cross each other. This point will most likely be offset from the true centerline of the chassis.

The Wilwood Starlite 5 hub and drive flange saves weight by using five bolts instead of the conventional eight. It also uses a lighter drive flange, and gun drilled studs.

tube and the same length of 2″ O.D., .065″ wall tube has the same strength, but the length of 2″ O.D. tubing weighs 1.4 pounds less!

Designing For Weight

Another design consideration is that the rules in most sanctioning bodies require you to weigh enough that you usually have to load your chassis down with ballast, so you have plenty of room to increase the strength and safety of your car without going over the weight limits.

As an example of this, late model dirt cars weigh about 1,950 pounds on average and the weight of the driver averages about 200 pounds, so that totals 2,150 pounds. Most rules require a car to weigh in the 2,300-pound range, so you have plenty of room to put ballast in the proper place. As long as you have this advantage, then it makes sense to add a few additional tubes in the chassis design to help make sure the area between the front and rear suspension attachment points is absolutely rigid.

Establishing Roll Centers

We try to establish our front roll center laterally as close to the center line of the car as possible, and about 3 inches to 5 inches above ground level. This is a critical area. If a roll center is too high or moves around a lot during body roll, the car is not consistent and handles poorly. What we like to see in a front roll center is the roll center staying as consistent as possible when the car is under braking and rolling to the right as the car goes into the corner. If it does

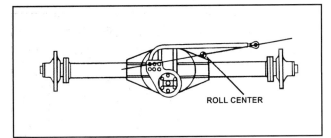

The lateral location of the rear roll center is the center of the Panhard bar. The roll center height is the distance from the lateral roll center to the ground.

The spindle design helps determine front roll center location, bump steer, steering ratio and Ackerman steer.

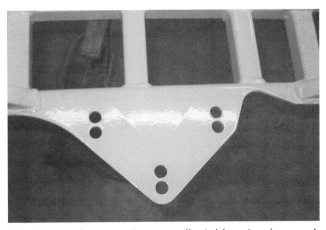

GRT cars incorporate an adjustable steering rack mounting plate that allows the rack to be moved back an additional 5/8-inch for increased Ackerman.

move around during corner entry, it should move to the right gradually as the car rolls. This will stiffen the right front to some degree and help the car get back on the left when leaving the corner.

A roll center that is too high will shear the front tire patch and cause a push condition. In our opinion, 5 inches is the maximum front roll center height. Some cars are built with a suspension that can adjust the front roll center height in order to adjust the car to track conditions. Being able to have a front roll center for certain track conditions is an advantage, but is not recommended for the amateur racer. We build our cars with a somewhat universal roll center that works well on most track conditions.

Rear roll centers can be anywhere from 10 inches to 16 inches above ground, and somewhere in between works well on most applications. Rear roll centers are established by the Panhard bar location on the car. All of our cars have the J-bar mounted on the left hand side of the chassis and it runs downhill to the rear end mount on the right side. Running the Panhard bar downhill at an angle creates what we call mechanical side bite. This induces roll into the

car not only with the roll center location but with the angle of the bar (see more details on this in the Rear Suspension chapter).

The length of the Panhard bar determines the lateral roll center and the severity of the roll produced. The lateral roll center is located half way between the two mounting points of the bar. The height is measured from the ground to the center of the bar.

The front roll center location is a lot more critical than the rear roll center because the front of the car handles 70 to 80 percent of the total rolling force of the car. Once the front roll center is properly established, the rear roll center height can be used as a fine tuning adjustment for the chassis.

Front Spindle Design

Front spindles need to be designed around the needs of your chassis. In the past we have used three different types of spindles with three different types of front ends. The current design spindle has an advantage in helping determine front roll center location because of the overall height of the spindle. In other words, the height of the spindle combined with the suspension mounting points determines the roll center.

Another design factor with the spindle is the steering arm placement. This helps determine several things like the bump steer

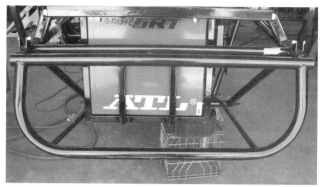

Crash zones are created by using structures like the front and rear bumper assemblies which are strong enough to hold the body panels in place, yet will deform under heavy impact.

adjustability, the quickness of the steering ratio (determined by the length of the steering arm) and the amount of Ackerman steer. (See the Front Suspension chapter for an explanation of Ackerman Steering.) GRT cars now incorporate an adjustable steering rack mounting plate that allows the rack to be moved back an additional 5/8-inch for increased Ackerman.

Establishing Camber Gain Curves

We like to see approximately one degree of negative camber gain per inch of shock travel on the right front, and we like to keep the left front as close to zero camber gain as possible. The left front camber gain is not possible to do and also have a roll center that you can live with, but you can get close. Trial and error is part of the design process.

Camber gain can be changed with A-arm length and location, but keep in mind that changing lengths and location affects roll centers again. So it's a time consuming process and is designed into our chassis for the best possible performance.

Watching tire wear on your tires from inside to the outside of the tread width can tell you if you are close on static camber setting. If you can't get your tire wear even on your fronts by changing static camber, then most likely your camber gain is way off.

Designing The Bump Steer

We like to see the bump steer on one of our cars at .020" to .040" toe out per inch of wheel travel on right front. The left front bump should be as close to zero as possible. These specifications are our opinion and we feel maximum performance can be obtained with these specifications.

The bump steer adjustments are made by shimming the tie rod end up or down at the spindle and the rack end of the tie rod. The spindle steering arm design and the rack mounting plate placement gets the bump steer close. If these two mounts are not close, bump steer will be extremely hard to set. These are the two main provisions we put into the steering design to make bump steer easy to set.

Building In Crash Zones

We now have a strong and light chassis, so we had to build in some forgiveness in the front and

rear sections of the chassis to help prevent the car from being totally destroyed in case of a crash. This also gives the driver an additional safety factor of having crush areas to absorb heavy impacts. Naturally the front and rear bumpers and right side door bars are braced good enough to hold the body components and take normal racing abuse, but they are light enough to crush on impact to absorb the crash. This in turn helps keep the main chassis from being hurt and helps protect the driver.

Crash zones are created by building a structure like a front bumper assembly that is very strong as far as holding the nose and body panels in place, but it will deform under heavy impact. It has a certain amount of triangulation using a smaller diameter and thinner wall tubing. For example our bumpers are made out of 1.25" O.D. x .065" and .75" O.D. x .065" tubing. These are relativity light gauge tubing and hold up well during normal use. In the event of a crash, however, this bumper will collapse and absorb much of the frontal impact. This saves the main structure and gives the driver a cushion of safety.

In addition to the bumper, the

actual front area of the bay from around the radiator to the front shock mounts should be considered a crash zone. There is no need for very stiff structural rigidity there. The chassis should have no triangulation there so it will collapse with relative ease in case of a severe frontal impact, providing even more of a crash zone.

The rear clip or tail section is designed the same way. It has 1.25" O.D. x .065" bracing and is built to absorb rear impact and not hurt the main structure of the chassis or affect suspension points. Some of the ways this is done is by using some of the bracing in the chassis just where it is needed. What I mean is the down bars from the top hoop are not run all the way back to the rear bumper like many chassis designs I have seen. This keeps the entire chassis from being affected by a rear impact because these two down bars are tying everything together. When you move these attachment points forward and use an under slung frame to build the tail section, it prevents the chassis from taking abuse forward from the attachment point of the down bars. Also, from this point to the rear you have a strong but very light and crushable box type structure that holds your body mounts, fuel cell, and rear bumper in place. In general what you have is a box that is strong and yet collapsible.

This same type of engineering is built into the right side door bar. It is built with 1.25" x .065" and .75" x .065" tubing so that in the event of a side impact it will collapse and cushion the blow for the driver, and have minimal damage to the main frame. This bar is as strong as it needs to be for holding the body and still is collapsible.

The driver's side door bars are another story. Safety is a key factor and you can't sacrifice strength here. Driver's side door bars must be designed so they hold up under severe impact and protect the driver. In our opinion triangular type door bars produce maximum strength (see photo).

Sturdy triangular type of driver's side door bars help to add side protection for the driver.

Crash zones should be engineered into the chassis to try to keep the structure of the chassis as raceable and repairable as possible in case of impact. Driver safety is the most important factor, and must be the top consideration.

Remember that these crash zones must be determined by how much the car weighs and the speeds that are being run. Heavier cars and higher speeds require that the crash zones be engineered differently with different sizes of materials.

Cockpit Safety Design

The driver's compartment must be designed so the driver won't injure himself in case of an impact or a roll over. You need plenty of room around the driver with no blunt objects in reach of him, plenty of head room, and door bars that are triangulated away from the driver for maximum side impact resistance. Think of all the ways that another car could possibly impact your race car, such as driver's side, another car landing on top of your car, etc. Then design the cockpit layout to provide plenty of safety for the driver in any type of condition you could imagine.

Design Is The Key Element To Being Competitive

The design of the car should be the strongest, lightest, and most functional that it can be. The design must have all of these features to be a winner. When you build in strength, you build in reliability. When you build in lightness, you build in quickness. When you build a functional race car, you have a simple, adjustable, and practical race car. These are key elements to a winning race car chassis.

Chapter

2

Race Car Construction

Construction of a race car chassis starts in the tubing rack. From there you must have a good plan to pre-cut and bend all of your tubing before you start constructing the chassis in the jig.

A good sturdy jig with removable attachment points is the best way to assure a quality chassis. You must carefully level the jig side-to-side and front-to-back. Pieces must be securely mounted to the jig fixture to hold firmly while you start to tack-weld the

Using a computerized tubing bender makes all bends more consistent, which makes every chassis more repeatable.

frame together. We usually tack-weld our chassis together in two to three locations small enough that when you run your main weld bead over the tubing, the tack weld is not visible. Starting and stopping the weld also should be done in a manner where the outer lap looks like one continuous weld.

Chassis Building Materials

Before we continue with the way to properly construct a chassis in a jig, let's talk about the types of materials we use. We have found that .083-inch wall Drawn Over Mandrel (D.O.M.) mild steel round tubing is the best for our application. Our 2 x 2 square tubing uses an .083-inch wall thickness also. Some customers prefer us to build cars out of a thicker wall tubing, and that is not a problem.

The grade of steel

that we most commonly use is 1020. It is not the strongest of the low carbon steels, but it offers all of the specifications required for a race car building application. The weaker grades of tubing bend real easy and don't have good return properties. Each number such as 1010, 1018, 1020, 1026, 1040, etc. designates how much carbon content is in the tubing. The higher the last two numbers of the four digits, the higher the carbon content of the steel. Naturally the more carbon content, the stronger the steel.

D.O.M. steel tubing is formed from a steel strip. It is electric resistance welded, and then the welded tube is cold drawn over mandrels to create a smaller diameter and thinner wall tube. The cold drawing process works the seam weld, making it virtually disappear into the metal structure of the tube. It is this cold drawing process that gives D.O.M. tubing a superior tensile strength and yield point over tubing manufactured from other processes. For instance, D.O.M. tubing has double the yield strength of hot finished seamless tube.

Also an option for building a chassis is using 4130 chromemoly tubing. However, we find that cars

MIG welding uses a continuously-fed wire as the electrode. This makes MIG welding very fast and clean.

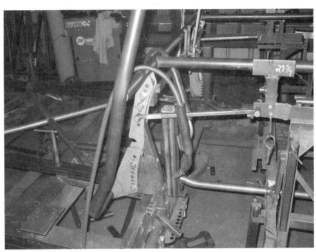

The chassis is attached to the jig in several different locations to prevent it from moving and warping during welding.

built with 4130 tubing are not as forgiving in crash situations. The D.O.M. mild steel tubing will give some and return to original position race after race. It is more ductile.

The 4130 material needs to be heat treated after welding to normalize the metal so it does not have an area that is weak or brittle. Usually the weak point will be the area right where the heat concentration stopped while welding. Also, the correct rod or wire must be used if you want to weld 4130 properly. 4130 has a lot more carbon content in it and therefore must use a rod with more carbon.

The 4130 material is stronger and more expensive, but not necessarily the best to use for stock car chassis construction. The mild steel D.O.M. tubing is best, provided the chassis structure is designed properly. This may not be the opinion of every chassis builder and racer, but GRT has currently produced approximately 3,000 late model cars with 95% being built with mild steel tubing,

so the record speaks for itself.

Welding Methods

Welding the mild steel tubing is relatively a simple procedure if you are using a MIG (metal inert gas) welder. We weld every chassis with a MIG and the welds are smooth and flow in well. The MIG creates a good strong weld and they are very adjustable for different types of material and wall thickness. What sets MIG welding apart from other types is that the electrode is a continuously fed wire. This makes its weld rate (the amount of inches of weld laid down per hour) very fast, and it is very clean — no slag is left behind.

TIG (tungsten inert gas) welding — also called heliarc — is something that produces probably the nicest and strongest weld, but it is a lot more time consuming and difficult. We use the TIG to do all of our aluminum welding and some of our fabricated chassis components, but it is not necessary to use on general chassis con-

struction. TIG is more suited for welding lighter materials like aluminum, and thinner pieces of steel. Welding steel tubing like that used for race car construction is a very slow process with TIG.

Some of the more portable welders that are small, like a mini MIG, work good, but sometimes they will not produce enough heat and don't penetrate well. So be careful about using a small MIG for this reason.

Welding The Chassis Together

The chassis is attached to the jig in several different locations to prevent it from moving and warping. We all know that welding pulls and warps the tubing being welded, caused by the welding heat. What we have found to work best is to weld the chassis in the jig approximately 40 to 50% complete. Then we remove all bolt-on jig fixtures and remove the chassis from the main jig. The chassis is then welded the rest of the way on the floor. We have tried to do this many ways includ-

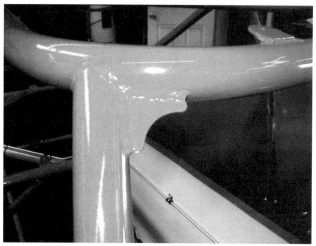

Triangular shaped driver's side door bars add more protection for the driver.

Gussets add strength to tubing intersections by spreading the load on the tubing over a wide area.

ing nearly welding the chassis all the way up in the jig. What happens when we completely weld the chassis in the jig is that the heat pulls the chassis so much that it starts distorting the jig mounting parts and puts everything in a bind. The 50% welding in the jig and 50% welding on the floor works well because it doesn't seem to get things so hot at one time. We tested this procedure and put the chassis back in the jig after completion, and found that all jig points lined back up approximately 99%. Again this may not be the opinion of others but it works well for us.

Another point about keeping heat and warpage at a minimum is the proper notching and fitting of all the tubing. Taking time to properly cut and notch tubing makes the welding job so much easier. The slag or excess material left on a freshly cut piece of tubing needs to be removed, and the fit must be checked before final installation of the tube. If this is done properly, the welding is so much smoother and quicker, and therefore making a nicer and cooler weld.

Gussets & Bracing

As the chassis continues on in construction, there must be a certain amount of gussets and bracing installed in high stress areas. Gussets are always put in door bar areas where driver safety is a factor, and also in the top roof area. This really strengthens the area around the gussets. In case a severe impact or a shear type hit is made, the gussets keep the roll cage tubing from ripping apart. They do this by spreading the load on the tubing over a much wider area. Gussets add a lot of strength for such a small area and so little weight.

When installing the gussets in the door bars, you have to consider the door bar design. Remember that door bars which are built in a triangular manner from the inside of the car out seem to be much more crush resistant. Some door bar designs are a straight up and down design and won't resist side impact as well. In either design, gussets help strengthen the door bar area, but the triangular design of door bars helps add more protection for the

driver.

A lot of racers put some kind of plate in the door bars to keep parts of other cars from piercing into the driver area (a lot of sanctioning bodies require this too). This is a good safety feature. 1/8 to 1/4-inch thick plate will be sufficient to provide protection. You can attach this by tack welding the plate to the door bars, or by making a bolton application. I have seen 1/8-inch thick aluminum plate used before, but this is not as strong as steel. Remember that when you are adding the steel plate on the left side door bars, you are also adding to the desired left side weight.

Sometimes brackets can act as a gusset or brace in the chassis along with doing their job as a component attachment. To accomplish this, your chassis design has to be thoroughly thoughtout.

Chassis Reference Points

Chassis reference points are locating points on the chassis that the racer can always go back to

To square the rear end in the chassis, the easiest thing to do is to use the links coming back from the 4-bar brackets.

The fuel cell should be mounted and supported with a steel tube cage fabricated from one-inch square tubing. The cell cage should be reinforced with a minimum of two one-inch square tubing bars in front, back, top, bottom, and both sides of the fuel cell.

Using underslung frame rails allows you to use ride height blocks between the rear end tubes and frame rail to easily set the ride height.

for checking the squareness of the chassis or the rear end location. These are real helpful in case of an accident or crash and let you keep records of squareness on the frame.

On GRT cars the front crossmember and the rear 4-bar brackets are perpendicular to each other and square to the chassis. To check reference measurements for various points on the chassis, install a string and plumb bob at the center of each inner pivot point on the crossmember, lower the plumb bob to the floor and scribe a mark. Then draw a line between the scribe marks. To determine if the rear frame is bent due to crash damage, measure from the front crossmember reference line to reference marks dropped from the 4-bar brackets on each side.

To square the rear end in the chassis, the easiest thing to do is to use the links coming back from the 4-bar brackets. If the link lengths are equal on each side, the rear end housing will be square in the car.

One other advantage of our car is that we have underslung frame rails and this allows you to use ride height blocks in between the rear end tubes and the frame. These blocks set the proper ride height distance between the rear end housing tubes and the lower frame rails. While the blocks are in place, you can check all of your square points with the car on jack stands. If someone crashes and they want to know if the frame is damaged, we give them measurements to check at different points on the chassis.

Fuel Cell Mounting

The fuel cell mounting in a dirt track race car should be as close to the rear end as possible and as high up in the chassis as possible. Normally the fuel cell mounts to the left side of the chassis. Fuel cells play a roll in handling and if you can make an adjustable mount, it makes it convenient to use the fuel cell for tuning the chassis. We will discuss this technique later.

The fuel cell should be mounted and supported with a steel tube cage fabricated from one-inch square tubing. The cell cage should be reinforced with a minimum of two one-inch square tubing bars in front, back, top, bottom, and both sides of the fuel cell.

Rod End Bearings

Late model dirt cars need to use good quality rod end bearings. We use aluminum rod ends everywhere on the car. They are lighter and do not wear as fast as a standard steel rod end, therefore they don't get as much slack in them and they last longer. The aluminum rod ends have a hardened steel ball and inserts that reduces wear. There are different grades of rod ends and we suggest you use a well known name brand. Check with the manufacturers or your parts supplier to find out specifications on rod ends, whether they be steel or aluminum.

Steel rod ends are fine but they require more maintenance due to the slack they get between the ball and the body.

In most applications, 5/8-inch rod ends are required for suspension and steering mounts, and are good for trailing arms and tie rods. 3/4-inch rod ends should be used on J-bars and steering supports. Rod end bearings used in shifting rods, power steering rods, or the throttle linkage should be stan-

This ATL fuel cell for GRT cars is designed to keep fuel forward, to the left and up higher in the chassis for more consistent handling and weight transfer.

dard 3/8inch or 5/16inch.

Aircraft quality rod ends are by far the best rod end. They are much stronger and have closer and longer lasting tolerances. For the serious racer with a larger budget, the aircraft rod ends are the ticket. In general we have found that a standard rod end is fine, but they do get slack in them faster on dirt track cars because of the continual dirt and sand. We

always lubricate between races because this is a big factor in preventing suspension bind. Also, make sure rod ends are aligned square with each other on radius rods, and make sure that the rod end is as close to 90 degrees to the attaching point as possible to prevent the rod end from binding or breaking during movement.

Chapter

3

<u>Front Suspension & Steering</u>

Designing A Front Suspension

What is used in most dirt late model front ends is a design from the Ford front clip with lower strut rods going forward. If you have access to a computer and use a program designed to determine roll centers and front end geometry, then you will notice that when you start moving things around it changes something else. Many of the design elements are dependant on one another.

Component Choice

When choosing components for the front suspension, you need to determine the weight, durability and safety of all of the components you use. First, remember that anything which revolves or rotates should be as light as possible, but there must be reliability and a safety margin built in. When you go past the point of reliability and safety, then it is too light.

A critical part that is too light is dangerous and not practical. The rule of thumb is always the same — any rotating and unsprung weight needs to be as light as possible. And, rotating weight is the most critical.

We use Wilwood's Starlite"55" aluminum hubs which feature an

all-new design focused on maximized weight reduction. It is a wide-5 hub that utilizes a five bolt design rather than the traditional eight bolt design. We also use lightweight drilled studs. The entire hub assembly weighs only 6.5 pounds per wheel, which is lighter than some magnesium

hubs, plus it is more economically priced.

We also use Wilwood's ULS-32 scalloped brake rotors to decrease overall weight and rotating weight. They feature a fully machined scallop configuration that provides the highest amount of weight reduction on a vented

GRT cars use an adjustable upper a-arm with low friction aluminum rod ends and a Howe low friction ball joint. The one-piece lower control arm is also mounted with low friction rod ends and uses a Howe low friction ball joint. They have more strut to tie rod clearance to provide more backsteer clearance.

Wilwood's Starlite 55 aluminum hubs and their ULS-32 scalloped brake rotors help to decrease overall weight and rotating weight.

Aluminum rod end bearings, lightweight steel spindles, drilled wheel studs and titanium lug nuts all combine to save weight.

Spindle design criteria includes spindle height, steering axis inclination, steering arm length, and steering arm vertical attachment to the tie rod.

straight vane iron rotor. Scallop machining removes nearly 33 percent of the rotor mass. The vented castings provide increased cooling capacity over machined steel plate rotors, and improved structural durability over drilled rotor designs.

Other ways to save on suspension component weight is by using aluminum rod end bearings, aluminum trailing link tubes, aluminum wheel hub nuts, and aluminum shocks that are mounted upside down. They are mounted upside down because the lightest end is the shaft end and it will be the one that is moving. Mounting it upside down transfers the heavier part of the shock weight to the chassis, which is sprung weight.

To save additional weight, we also use drilled wheel studs and titanium lug nuts. Spindles are made of lightweight steel and are gusseted well for strength. The spindle is one area where you don't want to get too light because of performance and safety.

Use the suspension components that your chassis builder recommends because they know what works and what is safe. There are other areas where you can save weight, but for the cost versus what is practical, these are all that we suggest you use. In other words, spending lots of extra bucks to get the components any lighter is not feasible for the type of racing we do.

Choosing A Spindle – Design Criteria

When choosing a spindle design you must look at what performs best in several areas. The steering axis inclination angle affects static camber and loading and unloading of the wheel during cornering, along with caster setting. The steering arm length and location determines Ackerman steer, steering quickness and bump steer. The spindle height helps determine roll centers due to the angle of the A-arms which are connected to

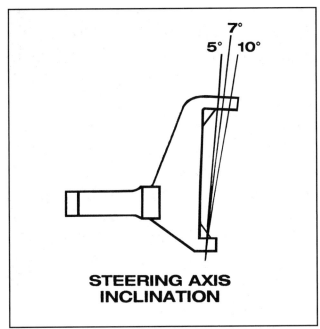

STEERING AXIS INCLINATION

The steering axis is a line drawn through the upper and lower ball joint centers about which the spindle rotates as it is steered.

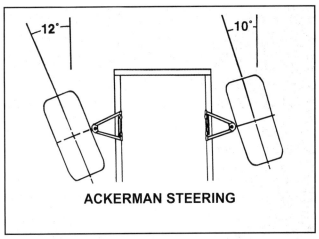

ACKERMAN STEERING

Ackerman steer is a steering geometry designed to make the left front wheel steer at a greater angle than the right front when the car is steered to the left.

the spindle at the top and bottom.

The steering axis is the line drawn through the upper and lower ball joint centers about which the spindle rotates as it is steered. The inclination angle of the steering axis is the angle in degrees between the steering axis and true vertical. This angle has effects on camber, steering and how much a front end loads and unloads during cornering. I've seen everything from 5 degrees to 10 degrees used on a dirt car. What we feel works best on our cars is 7 degrees. The more inclination angle used in the right front spindle, the more it will load the left rear when car is in a counter steer situation during cornering (front wheels turned to the right).

The caster setting produces this loading effect, but the more steering axis inclination present, the more it multiples the rate of loading the diagonally opposite cor-

ner. For an example of this, scale your car with the front wheels straight ahead and take a weight reading. Then turn the front wheels to the right 20 degrees and take another weight reading. The left rear and right front will have gained weight. If you want to do this comparison between a 7-degree and 10-degree spindle, you will find that the 10-degree spindle will produce a greater weight gain at the left rear and right front when the wheels are turned.

I have had drivers ask me to build spindles with different inclination angles for different types of tracks or setups. But we feel the 7-degree spindle inclination produces the best performance all around. Too much inclination angle makes steering more difficult, while too little angle makes the steering feel easier and have a darty feeling. The less inclination angle there is, the less caster effect

the spindle has. And, caster creates front end directional stability, so less inclination angle makes the steering feel lighter and have less steering stability.

Steering arms help determine the amount of Ackerman steer and bump steer in the front suspension. Ackerman steer is a steering geometry designed to make the left front wheel steer at a greater angle than the right front when the car is steered to the left. GRT cars now incorporate and adjustable steering rack mounting plate that allows the rack to be moved back an additional 5/8-inch for increased Ackerman. We have found that the additional Ackerman steering helps the car on corner entry and through the middle.

You can check your Ackerman with a good set of turn tables. Set the wheels straight ahead and then turn them 20 degrees to the left and to the right. Check the angle of both sides. One wheel will turn more than the other. This is the Ackerman steering angle.

Bump steer is affected by the steering arm's vertical attachment

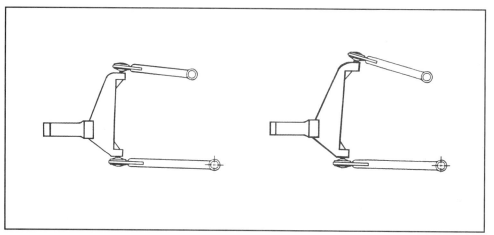

The spindle height helps determine roll centers due to the angle of the A-arms. The steeper angle of the upper A-arm (right) creates a higher front roll center, with all other factors being the same. The steeper upper A-arm angle also creates a faster camber change curve (more negative camber gain per inch of bump travel).

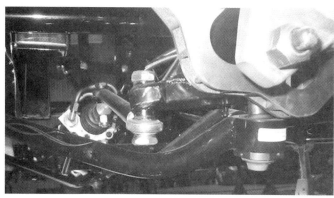

Howe Precision ball joints have the precision of a spherical ball joint with the misalignment range of a standard ball joint. They have more than 20 pounds less resistance than standard ball joints.

point to the tie rod. Bump steer is adjusted by placing shims between the bottom of the steering arm and the tie rod end. If the steering arm is properly designed, the bump steer shimming required will be minimal or none at all.

The steering arm length affects the steering quickness. The shorter the arm is, the faster the steering is. The longer the arm is, the slower the steering is. We have found that too short of a steering arm makes the car more jerky. It is harder to be smooth and this is quite noticeable on longer tracks like Eldora, Pittsburgh, etc. We have found that a steering arm in the 5 to 5.5-inch length works best and definitely makes the car

smoother.

Spindle height is the last area of concern. The height of the spindle determines the mounting angle of the upper A-arms. This greatly affects roll center location in both height above ground and left-to-right location. The height of a spindle must be taken into consideration with the layout of the entire front end design. You can raise and lower roll centers with spindle heights and move it left to right. But even though you get a roll center where you think you want it statically by adjusting spindle heights, you still have to work with the entire front suspension design to ensure that the roll center and camber change curve work properly during body roll. Changing spindle heights is a good way to work with roll center location without moving inner frame mounting points. Most spin-

dle heights range from 8.75 to 10.75 inches tall.

In designing our spindle height, we took into consideration our target roll center height (5 inches above ground) and lateral location (1-inch to the right of vehicle centerline), plus upper and lower A-arm lengths and inner mounting positions. All of these items must be considered together to yield a proper roll center location, and a roll center that does not move around drastically while the body rolls during cornering.

Spindle Materials

Once you have determined the spindle design you want, then choose the proper material. We firmly believe the fabricated steel spindle is the best system. When comparing cost, reliability and repairability, lightweight steel is better than aluminum. Aluminum is costly, bulky and doesn't save much weight because of the way you have to build them to be durable. Stay with fabricated steel.

Ball Joints

Ball joints are an area of front ends that sometimes are overlooked or neglected. We use Howe Precision ball joints for

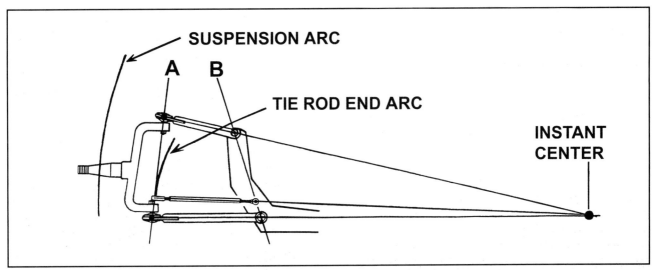

Bump steer is zero when the suspension arc and the tie rod arc are parallel to each other. To accomplish this, the tie rod length must fall between the confines of planes A and B, and the tie rod end's centerline must intersect the instant center. The tie rod may be laterally displaced so long as the length remains the same as if it were between the A and B planes.

both the upper and lower A-arms. These ball joints have more than 20 pounds less resistance than standard ball joints, which helps the suspension to operate much more freely. Howe Precision ball joints have the precision of a spherical ball joint with the misalignment range of a standard ball joint. They are rebuildable and adjustable. They have alloy steel ball studs that are coated for low friction and long wear.

Adjustable monoball joints are another option for use as an upper ball joint. But this is another area of cost versus what is practical. They can be used to adjust the angle of the upper A-arm to change roll enters, but again they are more expensive. And, if your car is designed correctly, you don't need an adjustable ball joint. The main thing you need to remember is that whatever ball joint you use, keep a constant check on them for wear and proper lubrication. This is a critical handling and performance

area.

Steering Rod Ends

We use aluminum 5/8" x 5/8" rod ends on our steering arms. They are light and strong. They make adjusting bump steer and toe-out easy. They don't bend like a regular automotive tie rod end, therefore they keep the front end more reliable and to specifications. Steering rod ends should be no smaller than 5/8-inch and a top quality brand. Keep them well lubricated (unless they have a self-lubricating liner) and check often for wear and slack.

Right Front Spring Rate

A soft right front spring rate is used to create side bite. If the spring rate is too stiff, the overturning moment weight transfer will shear the right front tire contact patch and create a push condition.

A softer right front spring rate will produce a quicker weight

transfer to the left rear under acceleration to get maximum forward drive.

Care has to be taken to not get the right front spring rate too soft. When the spring is too soft, the chassis reaction is the same as having the spring rate too stiff. It will shear the right front tire contact patch and create a push condition.

The baseline right front spring rate is 375 #/".

Bump Steer

Bump steer is the change in steering angle of the front wheels caused by the front suspension moving up or down through its travel. Bump steer causes the introduction of toe (either in or out) into the front wheels when the suspension goes into bump or rebound. Bump steer occurs when the tie rod end follows a path different from the path the wheel is following. If you visualize the arc created by the front wheel as it moves up and down through its

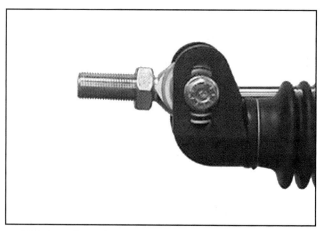

Sweet Manufacturing makes a rack with a slotted rack eye, which has three important advantages: 1) it allows the rod end to be more straight in line with the rack shaft centerline; 2) it is much easier to set bump steer by sliding the innter pivot point up or down in the slotted eye; and 3) the inner rod end is mounted vertically rather than horizontally.

When the inner tie rod end is mounted vertically rather than horizontally, there is no chance of bottoming out the rod end on the left front when that corner of the car jumps up.

travel, along with the arc created by the tie rod end, you will see that both arcs must have the same instant center or else the tie rod end will move in or out in relation to the wheel, causing a change in toe. If the arcs created by the tie rod end and the wheel are parallel, no toe change will be present. Bump steer results from the steering tie rod moving in a path which is dissimilar to the path of the wheel it is connected to.

Bump steer can be corrected on most cars by shimming the steering rod end up or down on the steering rack or spindle. A well designed race car will have no more than .015-inch of bump steer per inch through its suspension travel. We like as close as possible to zero at the left front, and .020 to .040-inch toe out per inch at the right front.

Rack And Pinion Systems

When choosing a rack and pinion system, you must determine the ratio you need, whether power steering is going to be used, and the type of rack and pinion you want. There are several different brands available and most are very good systems. We have used most types available both with power steering and without power steering.

We feel that it is best to use power steering, so this helps us determine the type of rack that we use. When you use power steering you must have a servo valve (which regulates the power steering fluid delivery). This is another component that must be attached to either the chassis or the rack. The Appleton rack has the servo attached to the rack itself along with the slave cylinder, and this makes a very compact and functional rack and pinion system. There are less hoses to run and less u-joints involved routing the steering shaft. These are all factors we take into consideration when using the Appleton rack.

Sweet Manufacturing makes a rack with a slotted rack eye, which has three important advantages. First, it allows the rod end to be more straight in line with the rack shaft centerline. Second, it is much easier to set bump steer by sliding the inner pivot point up or down in the slotted eye in any

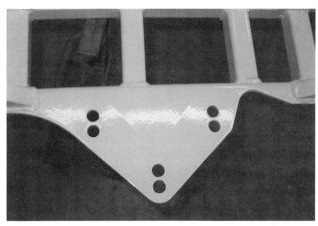

GRT cars feature two mounting positions for the steering rack. The forward position is the standard mount. The rear position increases Ackerman steer, which helps the car turn at corner entry and through mid-corner.

The Appleton rack has the servo attached to the rack itself along with the slave cylinder, and this makes a very compact and functional system.

increment required. Third, the inner rod end is mounted vertically rather than horizontally. This means there is no chance of bottoming out the rod end on the left front when that corner of the car jumps up. That saves wear and damage on the rod end and rack shaft.

Another choice you must make is the servo stiffness which makes the steering effort easy or hard. Most are offered in a light (easy to turn), medium (moderate to turn), or heavy (hard to turn). Most drivers that run our cars prefer the light.

The steering ratio of the rack is also an important consideration. They range from 16 to 1 to 8 to 1. Most late model dirt cars use the quicker ratio and it is standard production on our cars. The 8 to 1 ratio is also referred to as a 3.4 ratio. That number refers to how

far the rack eye moves with one turn of the steering wheel. The slower racks just don't seem to react quick enough for most drivers. We suggest you try different ratios and find what is most comfortable for you.

The mounting of a rack offers another advantage over other types of steering systems. The rack is easy to mount and most racks use the same three-hole triangular mounting pattern. They are mounted in front of the cross member centered in between the lower A-arm mounting points. The vertical location is usually mounted as low in the car as possible because you can always space the rack up with spacers if adjustments are necessary. The rack must be mounted with the center of the inner tie rods centered vertically with the lower inner A-arm mounting points. This

needs to be relatively close but not absolute because you can perfect the location with shims under the rack or in between the steering rod end and rack shaft.

The rack mounting position in the chassis can also be changed to adjust for desired steering geometry changes. Moving the rack up or down affects the bump steer. Moving the rack back and forth (left and right) affects the Ackerman steering geometry.

Chapter
4

Rear Suspension Systems

The rear suspension system is the most critical element on a dirt track race car. It determines how a car corners and how it is propelled forward. It is, in essence, the controlling element of the entire race car. For competitive dirt late model racing, there is no other choice than the four-link suspension system.

Four Link Suspension

The 4-link or 4-bar system is the suspension of choice for GRT. We have developed and used this sus- pension for 20 years. The 4-link uses two forward-facing radius rods on each side of the axle hous- ing attached to a birdcage bracket on each side. First let's talk about what a 4-ink does.

A four-link provides several advantages over other suspen- sions. It creates good forward bite because the upper link angles are mounted uphill. Any time a link going forward is mounted higher on the chassis than it is on the axle, the rear end is trying to go up underneath the chassis and thus the tires are increasingly loaded as the car is being pushed forward. This is because the upward- angled arms are reacting against the weight of the chassis which provides more tire loading. This is called axle thrust. The tire loading is an equal and opposite reaction to the upward pushing of the links against the chassis.

The 4-bar system is great for creating and controlling dynamic rear roll steer. Roll steer is the change in angle of the rear wheels relative to being pointed

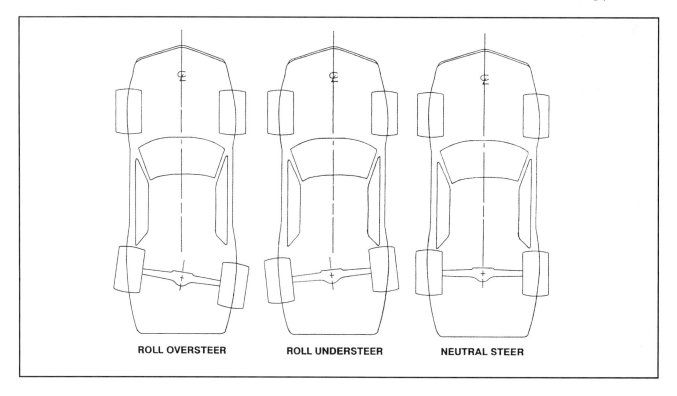

ROLL OVERSTEER   ROLL UNDERSTEER   NEUTRAL STEER

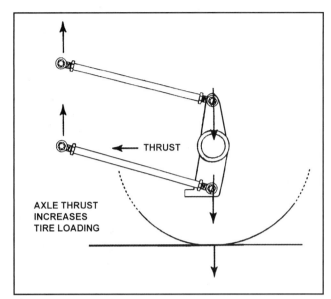

Axle thrust increasingly loads the tires as the car is being pushed forward. This is because the upwardly inclined links are reacting against the weight of the chassis, which provides more tire loading. The tire loading is an equal and opposite reaction to the upward pushing of the links against the chassis.

straight ahead. The 4-link system produces roll oversteer, which lengthens the right side wheelbase and shortens the left side wheelbase. Dynamic means that the roll steer is not built in, such as trailing the right rear with a longer trailing arm. Dynamic roll steer occurs as the body rolls during cornering due to the arrangement of the linkages that attach the rear end housing to the chassis.

The linkage layout of the 4-bar system creates rear oversteer as the car gains body roll. The right rear wheel is pushed back, and the left rear is pulled forward. This in turn helps the car turn through the corner. This really helps a driver to keep the car straight and reduces the chance of the rear of the car hanging out or getting sideways.

The third asset of a 4-bar is the indexing of the birdcages during body roll. Indexing is the rotation on the housing tube of the birdcages caused by the differences in angle and length of the upper and lower links. At the right rear, for example, when the suspension compresses during body roll, the coil-over mount at the front of the birdcage rotates forward. This pushes the coil-over mount upward against the spring and shock, resulting in the coil-over being compressed from both ends, which stiffens that corner of the car.

Indexing makes the spring actually compress farther than the rear suspension moves. In other words, say the car rolls over 2 inches. With the birdcage indexing, it is

The GRT sealed bearing birdcage is lightweight and produces no bind and no axle tube wear. It is fully adjustable with three radius rod mounting locations and indexing capabilities. Front and rear shock locations are available in 6 or 7-inch drops. The clevis-type shock mount eliminates shock end bind. The radius rod slots are on a radius so rod lengths don't have to be changed when adjusting rod angle.

The 4-bar system creates roll oversteer as the car gains body roll. This helps the car turn through the corner. The top car shows how the car can stay straighter with a tight condition and roll steer helping to turn the car. This is faster than the rear of the car hanging out or getting sideways.

4-link Dynamic Movement – Left Side

1
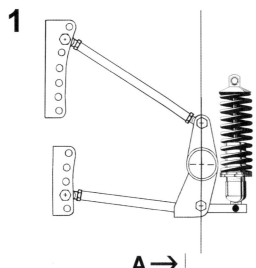

2

A→

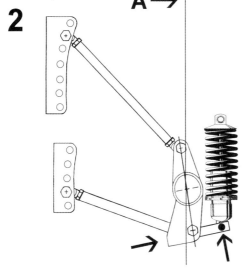

1. Left side links at static baseline angles.

2. Left side links during normal cornering body roll. Notice how the swing radius of the top link has rotated the top of the bird-cage forward, and the swing radius of the lower link has rotated the bottom of the birdcage rearward. This rotation is called index-ing. Indexing has caused the coil-over mount to rotate upward, compressing the spring. The net effect of the link angle changes has pushed the centerline of the axle tube forward (see A), which creates roll steer. Note the severe upward angle of the upper link. This adds significantly to axle thrust, which adds to tire load-ing and improved forward drive. This change in angle also signifi-cantly lifts the left rear corner of the car.

3. When the left upper link is set with more upward angle, the link gets effectively shorter as the swing radius rotates it down. Increasing the upward angle of the left upper link produces more initial indexing of the birdcage into the spring. It also produces more roll steer because the birdcage is pulled forward more. This creates more axle thrust and harder forward drive. Use more upward angle for a slick track. Use less upward angle for a tacky track.

4. Using less upward angle of the left lower link creates quicker initial loading reaction into the spring. It produces more instant forward drive. Less upward angle decreases roll steer.Use this adjustment when there is a minimum of traction in the track and the car is loose under throttle application.

5. More upward angle of the left lower link does not initially load the spring and shock as much which doesn't create as much for-ward drive. Greater upward angle does not produce initial drive but it gets the car up on the bars quicker. Use this adjustment on a tacky track when the car is tight under throttle application.

3
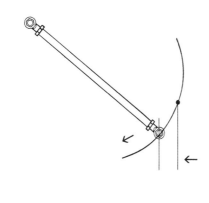

4
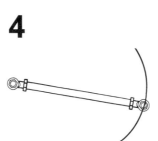

5

4-link Dynamic Movement – Right Side

1. Right side links at static baseline angles.

2. Right side links during normal cornering body roll. Notice how the swing radius of the top link has rotated the top of the birdcage back, and the swing radius of the lower link has rotated the bottom of the birdcage forward. This rotation is called indexing. Indexing has caused the coil-over mount to rotate upward, compressing the spring. The net effect of the link angle changes has produced no roll steer change on the right side (see A). Of the lower link had a static upward angle, roll steer would be increased on the right side (axle tube pushed back).

3. When the upper right link is set with more upward angle, the link gets effectively longer as the swing radius rotates it up. Increasing the upward angle of the right upper link makes the car looser from corner entry through corner exit because it creates more roll steer caused by the birdcage being pushed back. Use more upward angle on tacky tracks or tracks with long sweeping corners.

4. When the right upper link is set with less upward angle the swing radius path is flatter, so it creates less roll steer. Use less angle on slower slicker tracks.

5. The right lower link is normally set level. Notice how the swing radius in flatter (as compared to 6 and 7) as it moves up.

6. Setting the right lower link with more downward angle produces a sharper swing radius as it moves up. This pulls the front of the birdcage forward more which indexes the birdcage more and loads the spring more. This makes the car tighter at corner entry. Use this on a dry slick flat track.

7. More upward angle on the right lower link makes the car looser on entry because it does not index the birdcage into the spring. It also creates more roll steer.

1

A →

2

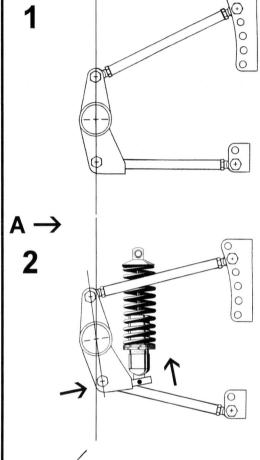

3

LINK EFFECTIVE LENGTH GETS LONGER

LINK MOVES UP

4

← RADIUS PATH IS FLATTER

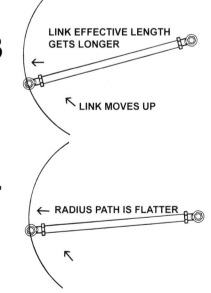

5

6

7

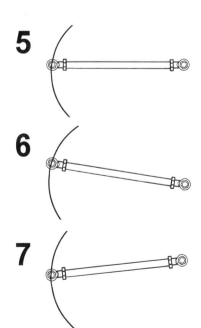

The GRT chassis utilizes 4-bar mounting brackets that have more adjusting holes placed closer together. This allows a finer adjustment of the mounting angle. The mounting holes are 3/4-inch on center.

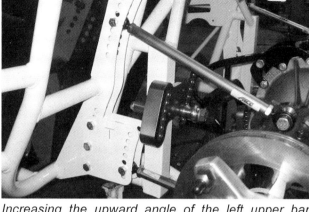

Increasing the upward angle of the left upper bar increases forward drive traction and increases roll steer. Increasing the upward angle of the left lower bar also increases forward drive traction and roll steer.

compressing the spring and shock at a faster rate than the suspension travel. So in turn you might have 2 inches of roll and get 2.5 inches of actual shock travel. This action is planting the tire into the track surface harder. On the left side, the bottom of the birdcage rotates back as the body rolls. With the coil-over mounted behind the axle housing, the indexing of the birdcage is compressing the spring and shock, which loads the left rear tire quicker and with more force.

For more information on how the 4-bar system works, see Chapter 5, Dirt Late Model Handling Dynamics.

Chassis Adjustment with 4-Bar Angles

The actions of the 4-bar suspension can be altered or changed by adjusting bar angles or lengths. For instance, reducing the angle of the upper link of a 4-bar suspension will take rear steer out and produce less indexing.

The upper links should be at least 17 inches long and be mounted with an upward angle of 23 to 25 degrees on the left, and 18 to 20 degrees on the right. Usually the left upper link will be mounted with 5 degrees more angle than the right. This helps to increase body roll and forward drive on the left side. With a greater upward angle on the left upper link, the left rear tire is loaded more quickly than the right under acceleration, which tightens up the chassis.

The standard baseline setup uses the 4-bar links angled as follows:

Left upper	23° to 25° upward
Left lower	6° to 7° upward
Right upper	18° to 20° upward
Right lower	Level

Changing the angle of each bar has a specific effect on the car's handling. Changing angles can be used to adjust the car to track conditions.

Left Upper Bar

Increasing the upward angle of the left upper bar increases forward drive traction and increases rear roll steer. More upward angle creates more initial indexing of the birdcage into the spring. Use this adjustment on a dry slick track when the car is loose under throttle application.

Decreasing the angle of the left upper bar decreases forward drive traction and roll steer. Use this adjustment when there is a lot of traction in the track and the car is tight under throttle application.

Left Lower Bar

Increasing the upward angle of the left lower bar decreases forward drive traction and increases rear roll steer. Use this adjustment on a tacky track when the car is tight under throttle application.

Decreasing the angle of the left lower bar increases forward drive traction and decreases roll steer. Use this adjustment when there is a minimum of traction in the track and the car is loose under throttle application. Work with the left upper bar before working with the left lower bar.

Right Upper Bar

Increasing the angle of the right

Increasing the upward angle of the right upper bar increases rear roll steer from corner entry through corner exit. Increasing the upward angle of the right lower bar makes the car looser on entry because it does not index the birdcage into the spring.

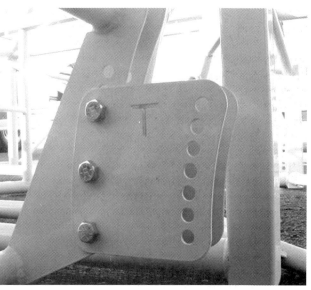

The standard GRT left lower link bracket uses a bolt-on bracket to accommodate a 15-inch long bar. This bracket can be removed when using the 19-inch long lower link.

upper bar makes the car looser from corner entry through corner exit because it increases roll steer on the right side. It moves the right rear back further and quicker. Increasing the right upper bar angle makes the car turn better under throttle application because it creates more right rear tire forward drive. Use more upward angle on tacky trcks or tracks with long sweeping corners.

Decreasing the angle of the right upper bar decreases rear roll steer and decreases right rear tire side bite. Use less upward angles on slower slicker tracks.

Right Lower Bar

Increasing the upward angle of the right lower bar produces more roll steer and makes a car looser at corner entry. Use this adjustment for tacky or rough tracks.

Decreasing the angle of the right lower bar decreases roll steer and tightens the chassis at corner entry. It indexes the bottom of the birdcage forward which loads the

The longer left lower bar takes away the instant hard forward drive under throttle application. It slows down the reaction to body roll and forward bite, and keeps the weight on the left rear spring longer. It makes the car tighter on corner entry.

spring which makes the car tighter at entry. Use this adjustment for slick smooth tracks.

Study the illustrations for examples of what is happening to a 4-bar suspension under compres-

sion and rebound. As you can see, the 4-bar is somewhat complex but very durable and consistent. What I suggest to you is to study the diagrams shown and build some type of 4-bar scale model that you can play with. This way

The limiter chain is attached to a clamp bracket on the housing tube next to the birdcage. This allows the chain to limit body roll without affecting traction.

you can learn what happens when you raise or lower a bar. You can benefit a lot from taking the time to do this. And once you have learned the 4-link system and know what changes to make to your car, you will have the advantage over your competition.

Using A Longer Left Rear Lower Link

The GRT chassis has an alternate suspension arrangement on the left rear that utilizes a longer left rear lower bar. The longer bar is 19 inches, versus the standard 15-inch bar. The reason for using the longer bar is to take away the instant hard forward drive under throttle application. The longer bar is works on all track conditions, but is especially good for tacky or rough tracks because the left rear does not push forward as much as with the shorter link. It makes the car smoother and more consistent under acceleration. It also makes the car tighter at corner entry.

When the length of the left

lower bar is increased, it slows down the reaction to body roll and forward bite. The longer bar keeps the weight on the left rear spring longer and doesn't allow the left rear spring to unload as quickly.

The longer lower bar slows the reaction of the left side, so the mounting angles of the left upper and lower bars have to be increased to maintain forward drive. In most cases the upper mounting angle is increased by 6° to 8° (for a total of 29° to 32° upward). The bottom link should be set at 13° to 18° degrees upward. If the car has too much forward drive, drop the left upper bar one hole. You can also lower the left lower bar one hole to get the desired drive.

When using the longer left lower bar, the left rear bite has to be reduced from 150 pounds to 75 pounds. This keeps the car tighter on corner entry. By increasing the length of the lower bar you can run more uphill angle and at the same time increase the top

radius rod angle to increase forward drive traction. This creates more forward drive using more bar angle and not with left rear bite (excessive left rear corner weight). Using less left rear bite makes the car tighter at entry, thus easier to drive. The increase in length of the lower bar also keeps the instant and massive rear steer from taking place.

Left Side Limiter Chain

Using a left side limiter chain eliminates the possibility of over-centering the left rear bars. Without a limiter chain, the body can get excessive roll and the left rear can drive so far forward that the bars will angle beyond their designed operating angles. This action can even bend the mounting tabs on the birdcage. The limiter chain keeps the left rear from traveling too far, which in turn helps the left front maintain traction.

To keep the birdcage from binding during rotation, attach the limiter chain to a clamp bracket on the housing tube next to the birdcage. This allows the chain to limit body roll without affecting traction. The top of the chain attaches to a tab on the frame.

Left Rear Spring Rate

The stiffer the spring rate at the left rear, the harder it pushes the car up on the bars. A stiffer left rear spring makes the suspension react quicker on throttle application. Adding a stiffer spring at the left rear also makes a car freer (looser) at corner entry.

The left rear spring rate should always be as stiff as the right rear, and in most cases, stiffer. In at least

The stiffer the spring rate at the left rear, the harder it pushes the car up on the bars. A stiffer left rear spring rate makes the suspension react quicker on throttle application.

The right rear double spring setup helps the car on rough and tacky tracks. A 200#/" spring is mounted on a real shock in front of the axle, and a 150#/" spring is mounted on a dummy shock behind the axle.

80 percent of all setups, the left rear spring rate is 250#/".

A softer left rear spring rate makes a car tighter at corner entry.

To make a car a little freer (looser) at corner entry, and tighter at corner exit, use a stiffer left rear spring (such as a 275#/").

On a very fast track or higher banked track, stiffen the right rear spring to resist the higher cornering forces. The right rear spring

rate is also increased on a heavy tacky track to loosen the chassis under throttle application.

Rear Spring Setups
Baseline

LR	250	RR	225

High Speed Heavy, Tacky Track

LR	250	RR	300

High Speed Slick Track

LR	250	RR	250

Right Rear Double Spring Setup

A 2-spring setup on the right rear helps a car on rough and tacky tracks. This setup uses a 150#/" spring mounted on a real shock in front of the axle, and a 200#/" spring mounted on a dummy shock behind the axle. The front coil-over is mounted on the bird-cage, and the rear coil-over is mounted on a clamp bracket. The front spring is holding the weight of the car at that corner.

With the front spring set at the correct ride height, the rear spring is preloaded 1/8-inch. Run the adjuster down on the rear spring until it touches, then run it down 1/8-inch more.

With the rear spring mounted on the clamp bracket, the axle rotation and roll loads the rear spring. This tightens the car on corner entry, and it makes the car turn good on throttle application.

Left Rear Clamp Bracket

Taking the shock off of the birdcage and attaching it on a separate clamp bracket is another adjustment procedure used with 4-bar systems. A clamp bracket is a coil-over mount that bolts solidly to the axle housing and is affected only by axle wrap up and not 4-bar suspension movement. Axle wrap-up is the rotational force of the rear end housing caused by acceleration.

When the coil-over is attached to the bracket, it only rotates as far as the torque arm moves up. With the spring and shock mounted behind the axle, this limited rotation of the axle won't let the left rear develop a hard forward drive. On short flat stop-and-go tracks this is important because it takes push out of the chassis so the car can turn under throttle application.

The left rear clamp bracket is only used in limited situations. It is used in conjunction with a straight Panhard bar, on short stop-and-go tracks.

The clamp bracket and straight Panhard bar help a car turn into a corner, and allows the car to pivot

The left rear clamp bracket is only used in limited situations. It is used on short stop-and-go tracks.

through the middle.

When the left rear is equipped with both a birdcage and a clamp bracket, it is important to preset the clamp bracket positioning when the car is scaled. If you don't do this, you risk changing the weight setting and corner height at the left rear when you change the coil-over from one to the other at the track.

When the car is being scaled, first get the corner weight set with the coil-over attached to the 4-link floater bracket. Then switch the coil-over to the clamp bracket. The static weight should stay the same. If it does not, adjust the height of the clamp bracket by rotating it until the weight setting matches the amount that was scaled on the left rear with it attached to the birdcage. This allows you to switch from one bracket to the other at the track and not change weight settings.

Brake Caliper Mounting

Brake calipers can be mounted in two different ways with the 4-

GRT cars have the brake calipers mounted solidly to the axle housing. Braking reaction forces are controlled by the 6th coil.

bar suspension — either on the axle housing, or on separate brake floaters on the axle housing. When a brake is attached to the floater, it will transfer the braking forces through a radius rod connecting the floater to a chassis mount under braking. If they are mounted on the housing then all of the braking force is controlled through the torque arm shock absorber, the rebound chain, and/or the 6th coil.

If the calipers are on a separate floater with a separate force reaction rod, you can adjust brake force through the chassis without affecting the main suspension.

Our newest chassis design has the brake calipers mounted solidly to the axle housing. We have done this to eliminate any brake reaction forces interfering with the suspension movement. This improves the coil-over indexing by making the reaction smoother. The braking reaction forces are controlled through the torque arm shock and sixth coil spring. We do not use the brake floater system simply because there is not a big enough advantage to have the extra parts on the car.

The swing arm suspension is used for rough or tacky cushioned track conditions. It is much smoother than a 4-link when traveling through holes and ruts. The part that is angled downhill and forward from atop the center section is a spring-loaded pull bar.

Swing Arm Suspension

A swing arm suspension uses a forward facing lower control arm on each side, a birdcage that swivels (or floats) on the axle housing, and a longer upper rearward facing control arm. The upper rear-facing links are 17 inches long, and the lower forward-facing links are 15 inches long.

The static angles of the links are:

Left upper	Level
Left lower	15° to 18° up toward front
Right upper	15° to 18° down toward rear
Right lower	15° to 18° up toward front

A difference between the swing arm suspension and the 4-link suspension is the mounting point of the rear coil-overs. With a swing arm, the coil-overs are mounted on the front links in front of the rear end housing rather than on the birdcage. This produces a softer type of rear suspension that requires slightly stiffer spring rates. When mounted in this manner there is no indexing of the spring. Stiffer springs are required because there is a greater motion ratio on the spring because it is mounted on a pivoting arm in front of the housing. This arrangement produces a double motion ratio and thus requires a stiffer spring rate. The baseline spring rates are 350 #/" at the left rear, and 325 #/" at the right rear.

The upward mounting angle of the lower forward-facing links helps to provide a slight amount of roll oversteer, though it is not nearly as much as found in the 4-link suspension. The upward mounting angle also helps to create rear axle thrust which enhances rear tire loading under acceleration, but it doesn't produce as much forward traction as a 4bar.

The swing arm suspension is used on real rough tracks. It helps the car through the holes and ruts better than a 4-link. This is because a 4-link will be continually loading and unloading the rear suspension while traveling through the holes and ruts whereas the swing arm will be much smoother through the holes and ruts.

The swing arm suspension uses a pull bar instead of a torque arm. The pull bar is a spring loaded torque link which absorbs torque reaction at the rear tire contact patches during acceleration. The pull bar is mounted at a downward angle to the front to promote more anti-squat under acceleration. This means the acceleration torque rotation on the rear end housing is reacted on the chassis by the pull bar and thus causes additional loading to be placed on the rear tires.

Because a torque arm is not used, something has to be incorporated into the suspension to control braking reaction forces. A reverse mounted 90/10 shock is used to cushion the braking forces. This is a shock that has 10 percent of its damping force in compression and 90 percent of the damping force on rebound.

The multiple fifth coil mounting holes on the torque arm provide different effective lengths. Torque arm length is measured from the center of the axle to the center of the fifth coil mounting point.

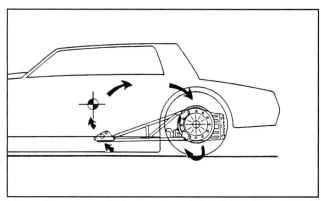

When the rear axle is free to rotate about its own axis in birdcage brackets, the power of this rotating housing can be used as leverage against the weight of the chassis to solidly plant the rear tire contact patches using a torque arm.

The stiff rebound (extension of the shock) provides the braking force cushioning.

Torque Arms

A torque arm is the most common type of torque absorption system used in dirt late model cars. A torque arm is a ladder bar running forward from the rear end housing ranging in length from as short as 32 inches up to 38 inches long. The most common starting place is 36 inches from the centerline of the axle. Torque arm length is measured from the center of the axle to the center of the fifth coil mounting point. What the torque arm is doing is absorbing instantaneous axle torque and helping transfer weight to the rear of the car.

The use of floating brackets (birdcages) on each side of the rear end housing allows the housing to freely rotate without linkage restraints. The rigid torque arm attached to the housing harnesses torque reaction energy and creates a controlled movement in response to acceleration torque. The power of this rotating housing is

used as leverage against the weight of the rear of the chassis to help solidly plant the rear tire contact patches against the track surface. This assists in hooking up the car and cushioning the rear tires so that it reduces the chances of shearing the tire contact patch and spinning the tires.

To shelter and protect the rear tires from violent shock reaction, a torque absorbing device is placed between the forward end of the torque arm and the chassis. A coil-over unit (called a fifth-coil) is placed into the torque arm system and allows the downforce to be more gently applied at the rear tire contact patches as the throttle is applied. I like to use a 73-6 shock (7-inch stroke, 3 valving in compression and 6 valving in rebound) on the fifth coil and a spring rate of 300 to 350#/", depending on track conditions. Softer springs seems to work best on extremely dry tracks and stiffer springs work better on heavy or "hooked up" tracks. Using too stiff of a spring rate initially will break the tires loose or shear the contact patch – much like having a solid

linkage attachment.

Torque Arm Length

Torque arm effective length affects how forward drive traction is applied at the rear wheels. A shorter torque arm length applies instant forward drive loading on the tires, but the loading will dissipate quicker as the car travels down the straightaway. A longer torque arm length will apply the forward drive traction to the rear tires more gradually, but it will keep the tires hooked up to the track all the way down the straightaway.

The shorter length is used for short stop-and-go tracks. The longer length arm is used for longer tracks and momentum tracks.

Braking Torque Absorption

Some type of device has to be used on the front of the torque arm for stopping the downward movement of the torque arm during braking. This is either a rebound chain or a sixth-coil unit. If the rear brakes are mounted to the

The fifth coil unit (left spring in photo) uses a 73-6 shock and 325 #/" spring for most track conditions.

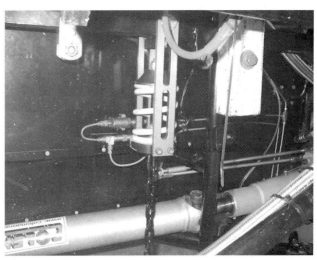

The sixth coil unit smoothly absorbs braking reaction forces at the end of the torque arm.

rear end housing (and not on brake floaters), the braking reaction at the end of the torque arm is hard and immediate, which bottoms out a chain very suddenly. Using a chain generally makes the car loose at corner entry. If a sixth-coil unit is used, the braking forces are absorbed by the spring and there is a smoother transition under braking.

The sixth-coil system cushions the rebound at the end of the arm instead of completely stopping the downward motion like a limiter chain. This generally will tighten a car at corner entry. GRT cars use the sixth coil as standard equipment.

A normal spring rate for the sixth coil for most conditions is 400 #/". This can range from 300 #/" to 600 #/". A stiffer spring rate is used to make a car looser at corner entry. A softer spring rate is used to make a car tighter at corner entry.

Torque Arm Bracing

Torque arms should be braced well to keep them from moving from side to side and loading and unloading the spring. A lateral movement of the torque arm could also cause it to hit the driveshaft. There are two different types of braces that can be used – a solid mounting or a floating mount. This is an important area and the choice of bracing system depends on what type of suspension you use.

With a 4-link and the roll steer associated with it, you need a brace that connects to the chassis and supports the end of the arm. This keeps the arm straight no matter where the rear end points. Therefore it keeps the shock and spring directly under the mounting point in the chassis and you have maximum performance at all times. This system requires the torque arm mounting points to float on rod ends at the differential center section connection.

With the floating brace system, the rear attachment points of the torque arm are bolted through rod end bearings to the center section. This mount keeps the torque arm

The torque arm brace connects the chassis to the end of the torque arm to keep the arm straight no matter where the rear end points.

rigid in vertical movement, but allows it freedom to move laterally. At the front of the torque arm, a tubing brace is bolted from the arm to the frame on the right side. This brace has a rod end bearing on each end. What this system does is force the torque arm to move in a straight up and down motion while allowing the rear end housing to pivot to accommodate roll steer.

The other type of lateral support

The GRT left side Panhard bar mounting bracket has multiple attachment holes in radiused slots. This means the frame side of the bar can be moved to different positions without having to adjust the length of the bar. The left slot is for a long bar, and the right slot is for a short Panhard bar.

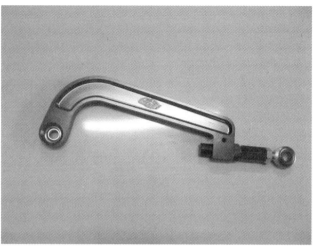

The standard Panhard bar is a J-bar that is 19.25 inches long. The GRT adjustable length bar can be adjusted in length from 18 1/2 to 20 1/4 inches without taking the bar loose.

system solidly bolts the rear attachment points of the torque arm to the axle housing center section. It uses a bracing bar that attaches to the front of the torque arm and triangulates back to the rear end housing tube on the right side. With this system, when there is roll steer the torque arm follows the path of the rear end housing and may swing as much as 2 inches left to right, depending on how much roll steer is achieved. This puts the fifth-coil unit at an angle during roll steer. This is not desirable.

Panhard Bars

Basically there are two types of Panhard bars — a J-bar and a straight bar. Both are used to accomplish the same thing — to brace the body of the car against the rear end housing so that there is no side shift of the axle during cornering. The bar is a lateral locating device. The Panhard bar is an important linkage because it

locates the rear roll center (both the height and the lateral location), and it can create leverage, depending on its mounting angle and location, to influence traction at the rear tires during cornering.

The J-bar design allows you to maintain a longer length Panhard bar and also have plenty of adjustment even with the driveshaft being in the way. J-bars are very adjustable. A normal mounting strategy is to attach the bar to the left side on the chassis and the right side to a pinion-mounted bracket on the rear end housing. This creates a downward angle from the chassis mount to the rear end, with a difference of at least 6 inches in vertical height from the chassis mount down to the rear end mount.

The J-bar is normally 19.25 inches long. This is our standard length and it works well with most track conditions. When the bar has angle in it, this produces mechanical roll in the car and

plants the right rear tire in the ground. This is extremely important on a dry track because a dirt car needs roll to maintain side bite. The basic rule of thumb here is, the more angle in the Panhard bar mount, the more roll that will be produced. And the shorter that the bar is, the more radical the reaction at the right rear tire. Cars that have a large amount of angle in the Panhard bar and are short will carry the left front wheel all the way down the straightaway. That is from leverage pushing on the right rear.

It is important to understand how the mechanical roll is produced with a left side-mounted Panhard bar. When a car enters a left hand corner and starts to go through it, the car's body tries to swing about the roll axis and shift weight to the right. At the same time this is going on, the rear end of the car is trying to go up under the car or to the left, the opposite direction of the body. Since the

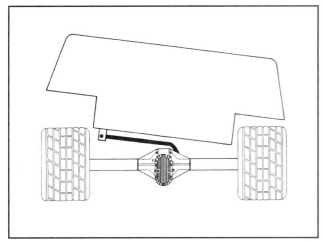

The short J-bar combined with its mounting angle pole vaults the body over the roll axis of the car. The overturning weight is transferred to the pivot point connection on the axle, adding more down force to the right rear tire. More Panhard bar angle increases left side lift.

rear end is connected to the body by a J-bar and the left side mounting point is on the chassis and is higher than the rear end mounting point, the body is continually rising up trying to roll and the rear end is moving to the left. The body in essence is trying to pole vault over the rear end.

Panhard Bar Angle

The Panhard bar is attached to a pinion mount on the rear end housing. This forms a pivot point for the sprung weight of the chassis as the body rolls during cornering. The angle between the chassis mount of the bar and the pinion mount of the bar influences how the chassis rolls about the pivot point.

The Panhard bar angle is extremely important in achieving body roll and left rear forward drive. More angle (between the chassis mount and the pinion mount) accelerates the process. More angle gets a car up on the bars quicker.

The standard baseline Panhard bar setup uses 7 ½ inches of rake.

The straight Panhard bar moves the rear roll center to the left so it loads the left rear more at corner entry and on initial throttle application. This pushes the left side down harder.

That means the center of the pinion mount is 7 ½ inches lower than the center of the chassis mount of the bar. This number can go up to as much as 9 inches, and as low as 5 inches.

The higher amount of angle (going toward 9 inches of rake) is used for flat, slick and slow tracks where side bite and forward drive are hard to get. If the car needs more roll up and forward drive, use more Panhard bar angle. If there is a lot of traction in the track, it requires less bar angle or rake.

A flatter bar angle (going toward 5 inches of rake) is used for tacky, higher speed, and good traction tracks. The flatter angle takes

The standard baseline Panhard bar setup uses 7 1/2 inches of rake. That means the center of the pinion mount is 7 1/2 inches lower than the center of the chassis mount of the bar.

A higher amount of Panhard bar angle is used for flat, slick and slow tracks where side bite and forward drive are hard to get.

The shorter Panhard bar is more reactive and induces body roll more quickly. It is best for a smooth, slick track.

The longer Panhard bar does not produce as radical a reaction in the chassis. It is best for rougher tracks, tacky tracks, or any track that keeps good traction.

away some of the body roll.

Panhard Bar Length

GRT cars use two different lengths of Panhard bars – 19 ¼ inches and 24 ¼ inches. The shorter bar is more reactive. It induces body roll more quickly. The short bar is best for a smooth, slick track.

The longer Panhard bar does not produce as radical a reaction in the chassis. It does not induce roll as quickly as the short bar. The longer bar is best for rougher tracks, rubbered down tracks, tacky tracks, tracks with a cushion, or any track that keeps good traction.

Straight Panhard Bar

An alternative to the J-bar style of Panhard bar is the straight Panhard bar. It does not have the J bend in it for clearance around the driveshaft, so it has to attach on the left side of the pinion. This moves the rear roll center to the left, so it loads the left rear more at corner entry and on initial throttle application. This pushes the left side down harder.

The straight Panhard bar should be used on short stop-and-go race tracks, or tacky, muddy tracks. It should not be used for slick tracks or momentum tracks.

Axle Dampers

An axle damper or 90/10 shock absorber is placed above the rear end housing and is angled uphill to the front of the car to help absorb braking reaction torque. In almost all dirt late model 4-bar applications, the axle damper shock is no longer used. This is because the axle damper shock resists body roll and weight transfer during cornering. It takes away from side bite and forward drive.

Setting The Pinion Angle

Pinion angle is a topic often discussed that has different opinions. I've seen several different angles on different kinds of cars. The best way to tell what you need is to check the pinion wrap-up under torque. The front of the torque arm on our race cars will travel upward 3 inches at 38 inches from the rear axle centerline. This is the maximum amount of travel that we recommend. This will enable you to see the amount that the pinion travels. We don't like to see the pinion over-center or start going up. Our normal pinion angle setting is six degrees down and this amount prevents over-centering from happening. From what we have seen, anywhere from 5 degrees to 7 degrees down is a good place to start.

The pinion angle is set to operate in a narrow angularity range in order to create the most efficiency from the universal joints. U-joints are intended to operate at a slight angle in order to preload the roller bearings. But more than normal misalignment causes high stress and wear on the ujoints.

As far as actually adjusting the pinion angle, it depends on what type of torque arm or fifth coil set up you have. GRT cars use a fifth coil torque arm with a sixth coil. The pinion angle is set with the torque arm flush with the bottom of the frame rails. Adjust the rod ends on the end of the torque arm as needed up or down to achieve seven degrees of pinion angle. Pinion angle is important so make sure you have this on your check list.

Differential Types

There are several different types of differentials available for rear ends. We have probably used every kind there is at one time or another, but in our opinion, late model dirt cars work best with a standard spool. I'm not saying that there is not a place for other differentials, but let me explain why we think spools are best.

With a spool you always know what the rear end is doing. It is locked up all the time and any of the chassis adjustments you make won't be affected by the rear end. Let's say the differential is not working properly and you don't know it. You make all kinds of adjustments to the chassis and the whole time it is the rear end is not working properly. All of your adjustments have been wasted. With a spool, you know that if you make a change to the race car, it works or it doesn't work, and a differential had nothing to do with the adjustment. With the various types of lockers or torque bias differentials, you always have a variable that could be the problem, but you never know for sure. On the other hand, a differential or locker offers advantages with varying types of track conditions.

With a Detroit Locker-equipped rear end, the inside rear wheel is disengaged and it rotates freely at corner entry. Under power, the Detroit Locker solidly locks both wheels together. The advantages of using it are eliminating corner entry understeer, and reducing the amount of tire stagger required to turn the car.

With a locker, you have mechanical parts that can wear or fail and this is the reason I have never felt comfortable with this type of differential. Lockers also add unsprung weight to the car.

A torque bias differential does not have as many mechanical parts as a locker. A locker has springs and cog type gears that act like a ratchet, whereas a torque bias differential just has gears that have close tolerances which produce the free wheel effect on corner entry. From what I have seen, the gears in those units can wear and this will prevent it from functioning properly. Keeping them properly maintained is a key factor.

Provided the differentials are working properly, the theory is that you can free wheel or let the car turn through the corner easier whereas a spool locks the axles together solidly and relies on stagger alone to turn the car. So as you can see, the torque bias differential would let you use a little less stagger. Provided the torque bias differential works properly, you can free up your car into and through the apex of the corner. Just make sure that if you run that type of differential, it is well maintained.

Proper Gearing

The car must be geared for the size of the track so that the engine maximizes its power range. If your car's power range is peaked at 7,500 RPM, gear the car so that 7,500 RPM is reached when you need to lift for corner entry.

Don't gear the car so the engine bogs down at corner exit thinking that this will help you keep the tires from spinning. This hurts performance in two ways. First, the car is lugging and not delivering the power that it could. When you get to a point on the race track that is slick, the tires will act like you are on ice. It is hard to control throttle response.

Secondly, gearing a car too high will hurt braking. A properly geared car will let the gear help slow it on corner entry and therefore you use less braking. We have learned through many races and test sessions that leaning toward the lower gear ratio provides better performance all the way around. Gear the car for the size of the track and the engine's power range versus its RPM range.

The car must be geared so that the engine maximizes its power range. If the power range peaks at 7,500 RPM, gear the car so that 7,500 RPM is reached when it is time to lift for corner entry.

Chapter

5

Dirt Late Model Handling Dynamics

In the last few years we have seen a quantum leap in dirt late model handling and traction capabilities. The evolution of the 4-bar rear suspension has completely changed the pattern of race car handling and track grip. These cars are capable of huge amounts of track surface traction, even under the most adverse conditions.

The 4-link system uses four individual link arms attached to left side and right side floating brackets (birdcages) on the rear axle housing. Through these links the suspension uses acceleration forces to increase the car's rear traction capability.

Under acceleration the rear tires are driven forward. This is called forward drive thrust. This drive thrust is delivered into the chassis through the upwardly inclined rear links. With the 4-bar links inclined upward, the forward drive thrust of the tires places a lifting force on the chassis at the point where the links attach. The resulting equal and opposite reaction produces a downforce on the rear axle, which increases vertical tire loading. The vertical tire loading then increases forward drive traction from the tires.

Getting the Car Up On the Bars

One of the most common phrases associated with dirt late model handling dynamics is "getting the car up on the bars." Understanding this is a key to understanding how the 4-bar system works.

"Getting the car up on the bars" means the two left side linkage bars of the rear suspension system are creating body lift due to the changing angles of the bars. The linkages lift the left rear corner and left side of the chassis which loads the left rear tire, supplying extra grip to the left rear tire for increased forward traction. The mechanical body lift and resulting vertical tire loading creates forward drive traction by planting the left rear tire into the track surface. The right upper linkage is also upwardly inclined, though not as much as the left in the baseline setup, and supplies vertical tire loading on the right rear tire.

The Panhard bar also helps to apply forces to the rear tires. The chassis is attached to the rear end housing through the Panhard bar. As left side body lift accelerates body roll, this force is applied downward at the point where the Panhard bar attaches to the housing. This increases downforce on the rear tires which increases the car's rear traction capability. The amount of downforce delivered

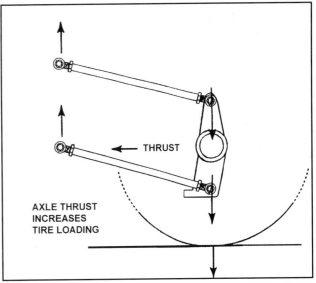

THRUST

AXLE THRUST
INCREASES
TIRE LOADING

The forward drive thrust of the tires places a lifting force on the chassis at the point where the upwardly inclined links attach. The resulting equal and opposite reaction produces a downforce on the rear axle, which increases vertical tire loading.

The linkages lift the left rear corner and left side of the chassis which loads the left rear tire, supplying extra grip to the left rear tire for increased forward traction. The mechanical body lift and resulting vertical tire loading creates forward drive traction by planting the left rear tire into the track surface.

by the Panhard bar depends on the mounting angle of the bar. More angle (from the chassis mount down to the pinion mount) produces more left side lift and more reaction force to the rear axle.

Rear Roll Steer

The massive amount of downward vertical loading on the rear tires creates great forward traction. But without some type of help, the rear end of the car is too tight to turn the car through the corners. To help the car turn, the 4-bar linkages create dynamic rear roll steer. "Dynamic" means that the roll steer occurs through changing angles during movement. The arcs created by the 4-links' inclination angles skews the rear axle. As body roll changes the inclination angles, the right rear wheel moves backward and the left rear moves forward, creating roll oversteer. This steers the rear axle which steers the car through the corner.

is experiencing maximum roll steer (making the car steer left). When the driver gets out of the throttle, the left rear corner drops, the left rear bar angles change, and the rear roll steer dissipates. This makes the car steer to the right. This can be a very unstable feeling to the driver. So, you have to make adjustments to the chassis that makes this transition slower and calmer so that the driver's first reaction is not to whip the steering wheel back to the left, which then makes it loose at entry.

An important part of making this transition slower and less reactive for the driver is to use a split valve shock at the left rear which is very stiff in compression. If you are using twin tube shocks, use a 9

The amount of downforce delivered by the Panhard bar depends on the mounting angle of the bar. More angle (from the chassis mount down to the pinion mount) produces more left side lift and more reaction force to the rear axle.

The amount of roll oversteer experienced is dependent on the angles of all four links, and the amount of body roll.

4-Link Adjustment At Corner Entry

When a car is up on the bars, it

compression, 3 rebound shock. If you use a monotube shock, use a 6 compression, 2 rebound shock with 200 psi gas pressure. This type of shock valving lets the left rear corner fall at a slow, steady rate.

The driver is also an important

part of keeping the car stable. The driver has to make a smooth transition from full throttle to braking to keep the left rear loaded. The driver should use a trail braking style of driving, which is to ease out of the throttle while applying a steadily increasing amount of brake pressure. A driver can't just pop off the throttle and stab the brakes. Staying on the throttle at corner entry (trail braking) helps tighten the car at entry.

Right Side Traction

The lifting of the left side of the chassis also assists the sprung weight of the chassis to roll over to the outside, which creates more side bite for the right side tires during cornering. More vertical loading of the right side tires stops the car from drifting outward or having a push condition due to a lack of right front grip.

A dirt late model car uses a soft right front spring rate. The softer right front spring promotes faster weight transfer to the right front at corner entry for increased track grip. As the car rolls over onto the right front, both the right front and right rear tires gain side bite. The right front will stay compressed all the way through corner exit. On slick track surfaces, a tie-down shock (soft in compression, stiff on rebound) is used at the right front to get the weight there quicker and keep it there longer.

Right rear side bite is accomplished with a softer spring rate and a soft shock compression valving. A softer spring rate produces more body roll. A softer shock compression valving allows the weight to transfer there more quickly. The right rear spring rate and shock valving are chosen

As body roll changes the 4-links' inclination angles, the right rear wheel moves backward and the left rear moves forward, creating roll oversteer. This steers the rear axle which helps steer the car through the corner.

Using a 9 compression, 3 rebound split valve shock at the left rear helps to make the corner entry transition slower and less reactive. The stiff compression lets the left rear down slowly which means rear roll steer dissipates more slowly.

The lifting of the left side of the chassis also assists the sprung weight of the chassis to roll over to the outside, which creates more side bite for the right side tires during cornering. More vertical loading of the right side tires stops the car from drifting outward or having a push condition due to a lack of right front grip. This setup illustrates a case of too much left side lift and/or too soft of a right rear spring rate.

A softer right front spring promotes faster weight transfer to the right front at corner entry for increased track grip. The right front will stay compressed all the way through corner exit.

Right rear side bite is accomplished with a softer right rear spring rate and a soft shock compression valving. The spring rate and shock valving are chosen depending on track conditions. When the shock and spring are too soft, and the track is tacky, the car can experience excessive left side and left front lift.

The shock and spring behind the axle on the left rear was developed in 1998 by Skip Arp and Joe Garrison of GRT Race Cars. This setup is referred to as "the hook" by racers because of the tremendous amount of forward drive it creates by being located behind the axle. As the chassis rolls during cornering, the top of the birdcage is drawn forward and the bottom rotates back and upward. This compresses the spring which loads the left rear tire quicker and with more down force.

depending on track conditions. A slower slick track will have a softer spring rate (such as a 225#/") and softer shock valving (such as a 3). A faster banked track will use a stiffer spring (such as a 250#/" or 275#/") to resist the high "G" forces encountered, and a stiffer shock valving.

Rear Panhard bar height also affects right rear side bite. The Panhard bar height establishes the rear roll center. A lower roll center height increases right rear side bite, which keeps the car tighter through all three phases of cornering.

Forward Traction Under Throttle Application

When the throttle is applied, the left rear tire drives forward under the car. This provides very hard forward traction, and rear roll steer to pivot the car through the corner. How hard and quickly this takes place depends on a number of factors. These factors include the left rear spring rate, left rear shock valving, whether a dummy shock is installed in front of the axle housing, the angle of the 4-

bar links, and the height and angle of the Panhard bar.

With a spring and real shock mounted behind the axle housing at the left rear, the driving force to the left rear tire is delivered almost instantly with throttle application. This works well on very slick tracks or tracks with no traction.

Adding a dummy shock in front of the axle housing at the left rear slows down the reaction at the left rear and the driving force of the left rear tire. It adds resistance to the suspension as the throttle is applied and slows down the indexing of the left rear birdcage. This configuration works best on tracks with traction or on momentum tracks.

Left Side Chassis Lift Limitation

When the left rear tire has forward traction, it will crawl forward underneath the car, increasing the angles of the left rear bars. As the body rolls over and traction increases, the top of the birdcage rotates forward, which causes the left upper link to push upward on the chassis, which causes the left rear corner of the car to lift. As this happens, the upward angle of the lower left bar increases as well, allowing the left rear tire to move further forward under the car. The more traction the left rear has, the more it will crawl forward under the car at the left rear. With good traction the left rear will continue to drive forward with nothing to stop it until the shock bottoms out. The more these left side links push up on the chassis, the more downforce delivered to the left rear tire.

A limiter chain can control excessive traction and roll steer. If the left side of the car can only roll to a certain point, the angles of the left side 4 links will not increase radically, and there will not be excessive body roll.

Adjusting Rear Lift To Track Conditions

If the left and right upper links are not inclined upward equally during cornering, the reaction forces are not placed equally on the two rear tires. If the left upper link is angled upward more than the right upper link, more downforce is placed on the left rear tire than the right rear under acceleration. This tightens up the chassis at mid-corner and corner exit as the throttle is applied. More left upper inclination angle is used on a slick track, or where more traction is required. If the left upper inclination is reduced and the right upper link angle is increased, that delivers more reaction force to the right rear. This produces more right rear traction, which is good for a tacky track.

The chassis can be fine-tuned with differences in the upper link angles between the left and the

The limiter chain controls excessive body lift and forward drive traction.

right, dividing the reaction force to the rear tires in any proportion.

Remember that the angles which affect the chassis during cornering are the dynamic angles. Dynamic angles are the angles which the links experience as the chassis moves in compression and rebound. Link angles are set or adjusted in their static setting (chassis at rest) in anticipation of how the angles will change as the body rolls.

More left upper link inclination angle is used on a slick track. This tightens up the chassis at mid-corner and corner exit as the throttle is applied.

Shock Absorbers

Shock absorbers are velocity sensitive, heat dissipating, hydraulic devices. The shock absorber offers resistance to movement of the suspension by forcing hydraulic oil through a series of valves and openings inside the shock.

Shock absorbers affect the handling of a race car as much as any other suspension component. Shocks are one of the most misunderstood and most overlooked aspects of chassis tuning. Most racers depend on someone else's recommendations when choosing shocks for their own race car. If the recommended shocks are incorrect, the racer ends up

The piston and shaft assembly from a twin tube shock. The heavy spring is a compression bypass spring valve. The holes in the piston are outlets for bleed valves and high speed jets. The milled slots in the piston control low speed bleed.

adjusting his chassis around the wrong shocks while trying to correct his handling problems. The end result is the racer turning in a mediocre performance.

We feel, however, that if a racer understands how shocks work and how they affect the car, he can use this to gain the advantage over his competition.

Twin Tube, Low Gas Pressure Shocks

There are two different types of shock absorbers used in racing vehicles — twin tube low gas

This cutaway of a twin tube shock shows the outer tube, the inner tube and the piston and shaft inside the inner tube. The space between the outer shock tube and the inner tube is the reservoir area. Visible at the right between the two tubes is the gas-filled plastic bag.

pressure shocks, and monotube high gas pressure shocks.

Twin tube shocks are built with two different tubes. The pressure tube, or center tube, functions as the cylinder base for the piston.

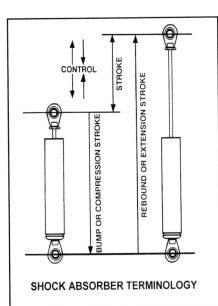

SHOCK ABSORBER TERMINOLOGY

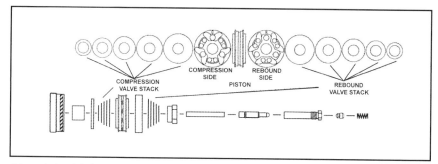

Monotube high gas pressure shocks use deflective discs for valving. The discs are spring steel shims which are attached to the piston. Fluid flowing through the metering orifices in the piston must deflect the shim stack, which uncovers other orifices in the piston to alter the pressure build-up. A shim stack resides on either side of the piston, so one stack is deflected during compression, and the other one is deflected during rebound. The damping characteristics are determined by a given amount of resistance at a given piston velocity. These characteristics are tailored by the shape, diameter and thickness of the steel shims.

The foot valve at the bottom of the inner cylinder of a twin tube shock contains two spring loaded valves. The one on the left is a blow-off valve that controls compression damping. The one on the right is a directional control valve – it pulls open under rebound to fill the cavity under the piston. The milled slots function as low speed bleeds to allow fluid transfer from and to the reservoir.

The reserve tube, or outer tube, provides the outer wall for the hydraulic fluid. This type of design helps to keep dents and dings from detracting from the shock's performance. The pressure tube is sealed along with the compression valve. The compression valve regulates the force needed to resist the compression of the shock. A series of valves and parts in the piston regulate the force when the shock is in rebound. The reservoir space between the inner and outer tubes contains a gas-filled plastic bag. The bag contains nitrogen, which is compressible and allows for fluid volume changes as the shaft moves in compression and rebound.

Monotube High Gas Pressure Shocks

Monotube high gas pressure shocks are designed differently from twin tube shocks. They have a single tube, they use deflective discs for valving, and they have a high pressure nitrogen gas chamber which is used to resist oil cavitation (foaming). The monotube functions as the inner bore for the piston, as well as the outer shell of the shock body. However, when the shock body becomes dented, the piston movement is hampered, thus resulting in shock failure. But, a benefit of the monotube design is that excessive heat from the oil transfers to the outer surface of the shock body more efficiently than in a twin tube shock, so heat is dissipated more efficiently.

A positive aspect of the monotube is that the design allows a larger diameter piston to be used since the bore is larger. This design also requires a second floating piston that is located between the shock oil and the

pressurized gas. The gas pressure is what creates enough force to control oil cavitation (foaming). When pressure on the shock oil gets low enough, bubbles will form in the oil as the piston moves through it. This diminishes the resistance force that the shock provides.

The volume inside the monotube shock is variable because the gas is compressible. When the shock is compressed, the shaft is pushed into the shock body which increases internal volume. The shock tube is completely sealed and the oil is non-compressible. So something has to give to accommodate the increased internal volume. What happens is that the gas is compressed.

When the shock is extended (rebound), the volume in the oil chamber decreases as the shaft moves out. But pressure still has to be maintained in the internal chamber so that bubbles do not form in the oil as the main piston is pulled back through the oil. That means there has to be

A left rear monotube gas shock should have 200 psi internal gas presure to help lift the left rear corner quicker under acceleration.

A higher gas pressure in the left rear shock gives that corner of the car more stability under deceleration. It slows the suspension reactions during transition.

enough pressure on the gas side of the floating piston to maintain sufficient pressure against the oil to prevent cavitation as the gas chamber volume increases.

Top performing dirt late model cars are finding new technical advances using monotube gas pressure shocks. In the past, monotube gas shocks worked very well on rough dirt tracks. But they didn't work very well on smooth, dry slick tracks. However, monotube shock technology has changed significantly. The change has to do with how monotubes have been engineered to work effectively with lower gas pressure. In the past, monotube shocks had a lot of rod pressure and rod pressure gain. This high pressure was a requirement to make the shocks work correctly. The shock pressure would actually increase the ride height of the race car due to high internal pressure. However, new advances in shock technology have allowed the monotube gas shock to operate properly with a much lower gas pressure level. With these changes in technology, the rod pressure has been significantly reduced, allowing monotube shocks to work well on dry slick tracks as well as rough tracks.

Monotube Gas Pressure Guidelines

Using more or less internal gas pressure makes a monotube shock react faster or slower. A higher gas pressure makes a shock react faster. Less internal gas pressure makes a shock react slower.

The following internal gas pressures are normally used with the associated valve codes:

Valve Code	Gas Pressure
4 valve	75 psi
5 valve	100 psi
6 valve	150 psi

When the track is extremely slick and smooth, the gas pressure in a shock can be reduced by a maximum of 25 psi. This makes the shock react slower. Any more pressure reduction than that will cause oil cavitation, which means a loss of damping control.

Left Rear Monotube Gas Pressure

A left rear monotube gas shock should have 200 psi internal gas pressure. This increased pressure helps to lift the left rear corner quicker. It helps to start the process of getting the car up on the left rear radius rods, which in turn will produce more forward drive.

Also, a higher left rear gas pressure gives that corner of the car more stability under deceleration. When the left rear corner is up on the bars and the driver lets off the throttle, the left rear can come crashing down. This action makes the wheelbase change drastically and takes the roll steer out of the rear end, making the car feel very unstable.

Using 200 psi gas pressure in the left rear shock makes it react faster on rebound and slower in compression. At corner entry, the compression resistance and higher pressure slows the reaction of the shock so the left rear corner doesn't slam down. At corner exit it creates a higher rod pressure to make the shock react faster to assist the car in getting up on the bars.

Left Front Monotube Gas Pressure

Gas pressure in monotube shocks can be varied to help tune the shock to track conditions.

Gas pressure in monotube shocks can be varied to help tune the shock to track conditions.

A split valving shock can be used at the right front to keep the right side tied down on a slick track or where there is no traction.

If a track is very smooth and slick, increase the left front shock pressure by 25 psi. This is like increasing the left front spring rate, which keeps the car tighter at corner entry. It also helps the car to roll up on the bars on acceleration.

Damping Stiffness Codes

Manufacturers of shock absorbers place a number on them to indicate the relative stiffness of the shock's damping force. This is called the valve code. The numbers range from 2 to 9, with a 2 being a very soft shock and a 9 being a very stiff shock.

In most manufacturers' numbering system, a single digit valve code (such as a 5) designates a 50/50 ratio shock. This means – theoretically – that the shock absorber is valved to offer the same amount of resistance in rebound as it does in compression. In reality, manufacturers valve their shocks to supply heavier resistance in rebound. For example, a typical 5 series shock with a piston speed of 6 inches per second will show 185 pounds of

damping force in rebound, and 140 pounds of damping force in compression.

When the valve code is designated as a double digit, such as 5-3, it is called a split valve shock. The split valve shock contains the valve code characteristics of the first number in compression, and the second number in rebound. For example, a 5-3 shock reacts like a 5 shock in compression, but like a 3 shock in rebound. This type of a shock allows you to tailor the handling and reaction characteristics at a particular corner of the car during weight transfer and body roll.

Split Valving Shocks

There are conditions when you want to use two different shocks all rolled into one. For example, you may want to keep a particular corner of a car from transferring a lot of weight when it rises up, which would require a stiff rebound valving shock, but you don't want to have a stiff shock for compression or bump travel at that corner. In that case, a split valving shock can be used. A split valving shock has one rate in

compression, and another rate in rebound.

In all split valving applications discussed in this book, the first number will always be the compression valving code, and the second number will always be the rebound valving code. This is consistent with most manufacturers' shock part numbering system. However, Carerra shocks are numbered just the opposite – the first number is rebound valving, and the second is compression.

Tie Down Shocks

A shock that is stiff on rebound valving and softer on compression valving is called a "tie down" shock. It keeps the corner of the car where it is attached tied down, making it hard for the body to rise up at that corner.

Dirt late model handling dynamics uses shocks that hold the car up on the left rear and down on the right front and right rear. In most cases split valving shocks are used to accomplish this. Holding the chassis down on the right side helps to create side bite.

Use a 3-5 (3 compression, 5

Shock control at low piston speeds affects how the race car handles through the corners, while medium and high speed control affects how the race car handles when it encounters bumps and ruts.

A 9-3 shock, such as used at the left rear, is an example of an "easy up" shock. The soft 3 rebound valving allows the shock to quickly and easily extend.

rebound) shock or a 4-6 (4 compression, 6 rebound) shock at the right front to keep the right side tied down on a slick track or where there is no traction. The stiffer rebound valving keeps the weight loaded on the right front longer and stops it from loading the left rear too quickly.

Not only does keeping the right side tied down create side bite, but it also helps to keep the left side up so the left rear will not compress quickly. When the car is up on the bars there is a lot of rear steer, so you want to keep the left rear up so the rear steer doesn't change quickly.

Easy Up Shocks

The opposite of a tie-down shock is an "easy up" shock, such as a 9-3. It has a rebound damping (3) that is soft, and a compression (9) that is a very stiff valving. The 9-3 split valve shock is used at the left rear to help the car get up on the bars and keep it there. The soft 3 rebound valving allows the shock to quickly and easily extend. The stiff 9 compression valving keeps the left rear extended. This is especially important at corner entry so that the left rear corner doesn't drop rapidly and change the rear steer quickly.

How Shocks Influence Handling

Inside shocks, there are a series of valves and orifices, or deflective discs. When the shaft and piston assembly move, they force fluid through these. This creates a resistance to movement. Shocks will produce a resistance force which is proportional to the speed of the shaft movement. When compressed slowly, a shock generates less resistance force than when it is moved faster. This prin-

ciple is used to create different levels, or stages, of resistance force. This staged valving is necessary because the shock resistance required to control the race car suspension when it goes over a severe bump (referred to as high speed control) is much greater than the resistance needed to control body roll or the suspension movement caused by small bumps (referred to as low or medium speed control). Shock resistance at low, medium, and high piston speeds must be matched to the needs of the race car.

In the simplest terms, racing shocks perform two functions:

1. When bumps and ruts are encountered, shocks keep the chassis settled and the tires in compliance with the race track. Without shocks, the chassis would pitch, roll, and bounce violently whenever the race car encounters bumps and ruts. The tires could lose contact with the track surface.

2. Shocks help control the rate

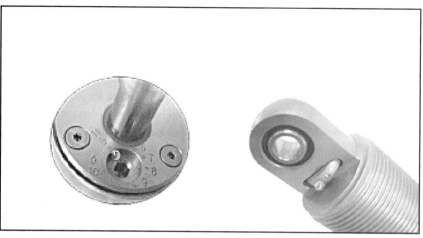

Adjustable shocks provide the racer a cost savings because a wide range of split valve shocks are not required. On this double adjustable shock by PRO, compression is adjusted by turning the thumbwheel (above right). Rebound valving stiffness is chosen by rotating the adjuster slot (above left).

of chassis roll and pitch caused by dynamic weight transfer. Whenever a race car accelerates, decelerates, or corners, the chassis will pitch or roll (due to weight transfer). Without shocks, body roll and pitch would be violent and the chassis would not be stable.

Shock control at low piston speeds affects how the race car handles through the corners, while medium and high speed control affects how the race car handles whenever it encounters bumps and ruts.

Rebound control is a shock's resistance to extending and is specified at a given piston speed. The amount of rebound control developed by a shock will determine, generally, how quickly a tire is unloaded during dynamic weight transfer, and how quickly the suspension "rebounds" or returns to its original position, after the spring has been compressed.

Compression, or bump control, is a shock's resistance to compression and is specified at a given piston speed. Compression control

will determine, generally, how quickly a tire is loaded during dynamic weight transfer and how the suspension will react whenever a bump is initially contacted.

The stiffness of the shock absorbers used on a race car has a profound effect on the rate at which weight transfer affects the loads on the tires. The "rate" of weight transfer means how quickly or slowly a particular shock valving allows weight to transfer. Because of this, shocks are a very important factor when it comes to handling. Basically, soft shocks allow weight transfer to affect tire loadings more quickly than stiff shocks.

There really is no mystery to shock function and tuning. However, there are complexities and qualities that need to be considered when choosing shocks for a specific application. By keeping this basic information in mind you should be able to install the correct shocks for each situation when troubleshooting handling problems. This should also enable you to have the confidence to

make changes with fairly good expectations of results.

Above all, remember that chassis tuning is a compromise and shocks, though a very important part of the setup, are still only a part. Keep the following in mind for proper chassis tuning:

1. As the piston speed of a shock increases, the shock gets stiffer.

2. Large bumps hit at high speeds cause the highest piston velocities, and the highest shock resistance, to occur.

3. The low speed resistance of a shock absorber controls the rate of body roll and pitch, and also how quickly a tire is loaded and unloaded during dynamic weight transfer.

4. Generally, soft shocks will cause a tire to become loaded or unloaded (due to dynamic weight transfer) more quickly than stiff shocks.

Adjustable Rate Double Tube Shocks

Several of the manufacturers of double tube shocks offer an externally adjustable shock absorber. Some are adjustable in rebound, some are adjustable in both rebound and compression. All use different methods to accomplish the adjustments.

Adjustable shocks provide the racer a cost savings because a wide range of split valve shocks are not required. One or two different shocks per corner are all that is required to fine tune the handling of the race car. This makes changes much simpler and quicker at the track as well. All that is required is to turn an adjusting knob instead of changing shocks.

Matching Shocks to Track Conditions

When you choose a shock valving, make sure you consider the surface to be run on. Too stiff of a valving will more or less let a wheel skate over bumps, and the tire won't stay on the ground, thus loosing traction and speed. The same goes for a shock that does not have stiff enough valving. The wheel will bounce at an excessive rate and not stay in contact with the surface. Again it looses traction and control.

Let me give you some examples of which shocks we normally run on our late models. A standard setup uses a 75 valving shock on both the left front and right front. Our rear shocks use a 94 valving shock at both the left rear and right rear corner. This particular shock combination works well on most track conditions that are fairly smooth, and flat to semi-banked. I like to see a racer use these shocks until the track becomes rough, has a cushion, is extremely high banked, or is extremely flat and dry slick with slow corner speeds. When a track starts to get slick, change to a 99-3 shock at the left rear (mounted behind the axle tube). This helps to get the car up on the bars on the left side quicker to enhance forward drive traction.

When the track is wet or heavy or very tacky, mount the left rear 94 shock in front of the rear axle housing and mount the coil spring on a dummy shock behind the axle. This takes away from the instantaneous forward drive under acceleration and keeps the rear of the car freer so it turns good through mid-corner and corner exit.

Shocks To Match Track Conditions

Baseline

LF	75	RF	75
LR	99-3	RR	94

Banked and/or High Speed Track

LF	75	RF	76
LR	99-3	RR	94

Very Slick or Slow Track

LF	75	RF	74-6
LR	99-3	RR	93

Very Tacky Track

LF	75	RF	75
LR	94	RR	94

On a slow flat track that is slick, use a 73-5 right front shock The softer compression valving helps to accelerate weight transfer to the right front, and the stiffer rebound valving keeps weight on the right front longer, which helps right front side bite and grip.

If the track is high banked and/or has a cushion, we generally change to a 76 right front shock. This is a stiffer valved shock which helps stabilize the car for these types of track conditions.

A real slow flat track that is slick can use a 73-5 right front shock. The softer compression valving helps to accelerate weight transfer to the right front, and the stiffer rebound valving keeps weight on the right front longer, which helps right front side bite and grip. A 3 valving shock is used at the right rear. The softer valving shock accelerates body roll for faster weight transfer to the right rear.

A dummy shock is usually used in front of the rear axle at the left rear corner. It is used to slow down suspension reaction time.

This helps gain side bite and forward traction. If a monotube shock is being used, and it is difficult to get side bite, reduce gas pressure by 25 PSI in the right rear shock.

High Speed/High Banked Track Setup

On a high speed and/or high banked track, the right front shock has to offer more resistance in compression. With twin tube shocks, use a 76 shock instead of a 75.

If you use monotube shocks, use a 76 shock with 100 PSI gas pressure, or a 75 shock with 150 PSI pressure. The 75 shock with increased gas pressure will act as if it was in between a 75 and 76 valving. Adding gas pressure slows down the reaction time of a shock, just the same as stiffening the valving of a shock.

Chassis Adjustment with Shocks – Loose At Corner Entry

If a car is loose at corner entry, you can stiffen the compression valving of the left front shock. Use a 6-5 shock. This has the same effect as using a stiffer spring, but it will not affect the right rear corner at exit.

Dummy Shock

A "dummy" shock is a shock absorber which is designed to have no force resistance during movement. These shocks are manufactured with a valve code designation of "0." In the old days, racers would create their own dummy shock by drilling a hole in a twin tube shock and draining out the fluid. But running a shock without fluid will quickly make it lock up.

A dummy shock is usually used in front of the rear axle at the left

rear corner. It is used to slow down suspension reaction time. Even though it has a zero damping force, it still offers some resistance. Using a dummy shock in front of the birdcage at the left rear takes some of the instantaneous forward drive traction out of the car. The car will not be as quick getting up on the left rear.

Shock Dyno Testing

Not all shocks are made the same. There are manufacturing tolerances involved when building and assembling the precise parts that go into shocks. Chances are that if you pull four of the same part number of any brand of shock off the shelf, and dyno test them, you will find small variations in the compression and rebound curves between each. This is normal. You will also find that most shocks labeled as a 50/50 ratio actually have more damping force in rebound. This could present a problem when you are looking for a particular chassis tuning effect from a shock.

However there is a solution to this problem. We have each shock we use dyno tested by the manufacturer, and we keep those sheets with each shock. This enables us to refer to each dyno sheet to get exact damping velocity specifications, and it provides a base of comparison between different shocks. You know what you are putting on the car and can tune your car easier and much more effectively.

A shock dynamometer is a machine that measures a shock absorber's function. It is used to identify and evaluate the damping characteristics of the particular shock being tested.

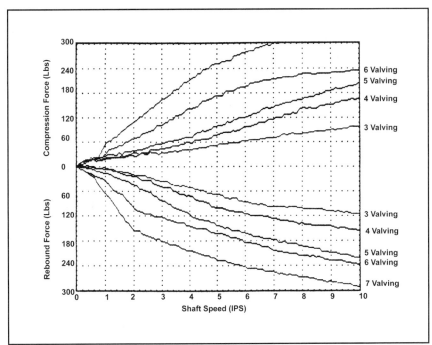

This is a shock dyno graph of a double adjustable twin tube shock. The rebound and compression curves for each valving code are integrated together on one sheet for a comparison of the damping capabilities of each. The graph lines are jagged because the shock force is tested at each increment of shaft speed, not just at four or five speeds.

There are many different types of shock dynos. This is a very sophisticated dyno that measures hundreds of samples during the test. It shows the acceleration curve exactly the same as the shock sees it on a chassis.

Shock dynos are sophisticated machines. They are attached to computers to aid in the evaluation of resistance force versus piston speed. Damping forces (in pounds of force) are measured at several different piston speeds, from slow to fast. Charting how many pounds of force a shock generates at certain piston speeds (measured in inches per second) can demonstrate how the shock will affect the handling of the race car. Charting force versus piston speed will show curves that influence control characteristics at various piston velocities. For a simulation of body roll and weight transfer during cornering, shocks are generally tested at a velocity of 4.7 inches per second, which will show the damping characteristics of the low speed valving.

Get dyno sheets from your shock manufacturer on each of your shocks (they may charge a small fee for this). Also, have your shocks dyno tested periodically because you can't tell if there may be an internal problem.

Tires & Wheels

Tire Selection

Tire selection is one of the most important factors in finishing the race car setup and delivering it to the ground. Choosing the proper tire along with tire compound, tread design, grooving and siping patterns and sidewall stiffness are all factors to aid traction and performance.

Tire Compound Choice

You can choose from a variety of compounds from very soft to very hard. The proper tire hardness is determined by the track conditions. On dirt tracks, conditions can change greatly during the night from the beginning of hot laps to the feature race. Therefore sometimes you must choose a compound that will be effective at the end of the race. It may not be as fast early in the evening, but if you choose one that is too soft, you won't be in the ball park at the end.

If you question whether your compound choice will be too soft or too hard, always lean toward being a little too hard rather than too soft. A harder compound tire will be there at the end, whereas a softer one may give up.

In most cases, soft tires are used for qualifying, heat races, wet tracks, or tracks that don't have a lot of abrasion. Softer tires can also be used on harder tracks that don't build a lot of heat in the tires, or that have loose surface dirt. You will also notice that softer tires wear at a faster rate and will tear or rip easily. This is something you have to take into consideration when you use a soft tire. You have to learn how long the tire is going to do it's job on a particular race track condition.

The more you groove and/or sipe a tire, the faster a softer tire will start wearing. This is usually the reason that grooving and siping works well on a tire for qualifying and/or short heat races. It helps the tire get a bite. Tracks that have moisture in them and are packed well may not require as much tire grooving. If the track has loose dirt on it that is not packed down, grooving the tire more will increase traction.

Tracks that have a lot of rocks or pebbles promote wear at a more rapid pace, so take this into consideration when choosing a tire compound. This type of track is

Tire selection is one of the most important factors in finishing the race car setup and delivering it to the ground. Choosing the proper tire along with tire compound, tread design, grooving and siping patterns and sidewall stiffness are all factors to aid traction and performance.

Tire Compound Hardness Comparison
Goodyear vs Hoosier

Goodyear Compound	Hoosier Compound
M100	D03
M200	D11
M300	D21
M400	D55

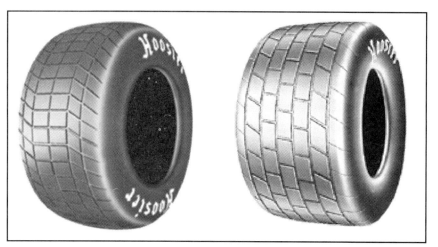

Two of the most widely used tread patterns are the checkerboard (left) and the stagger block (right).

going to be hard or abrasive, so this will require a harder compound tire. A track that packs down and develops an asphalt type of surface will also require a harder compound.

A race track that is hard but yet doesn't get abrasive or build a lot of heat in the tires might require some tire grooving or siping. A track like this will sometimes require a hard compound tire. This in turn might cause a tire to slick over or glaze. When you groove a tire, it helps the tire dig into a hard surface and helps prevent glazing. Grooving and siping add flexibility to the tread blocks, which helps prevent the glazing problem.

Watch track conditions closely. If you are not familiar with how a track might change, find out from people who race there regularly. When you choose your compound, whether it be hard, soft, or somewhere in between, if there is a doubt about which one to use, go with the harder of the possibilities.

Tire Tread Patterns

Tread patterns on tires are usually formed in some sort of block or chain link configuration. These tread designs work well on average conditions. Other tire tread patterns that are used include a "rain tread" similar to a street tire, and a circle groove, which has multiple grooves around the circumference of the tires.

The tires with the block type of pattern need less grooving than a circle groove tire. But, in most conditions, all tires will need some kind of grooving or siping to promote traction. The only time you would not want any additional grooving would be on a hard asphalt type of track that is abrasive. On that type of track, you need as much rubber on the tire as possible to grip the track.

Tire Grooving & Siping

Once you understand the track conditions, you must decide how many extra grooves and sipes to put in a tire. Nobody really likes to groove and sipe tires, but it is a job that is required to make a car fast and competitive.

Before you start, make sure you have the proper equipment to do the job correctly. Good grooving irons are a must and make the job so much easier. To do the job correctly, you need an adjustable grooving iron which can be set to various temperatures. The groover we use is called a Rillfit IV and it is the "Cadillac" of all grooving irons. This particular grooving iron doesn't apply the heat until you actually push the groover through the tire. As you push the blades through the rubber, it cuts the groove while the fresh rubber ahead of the grooving iron keeps the blade cool enough so it does not get red hot and break a blade.

When working with a conventional groover, or setting blade depths, be extremely cautious not to burn yourself. It takes a long time to cool off after you unplug it, so don't lay one around where

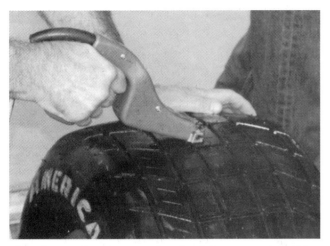

Good grooving irons make the job so much easier. Before starting, make sure the tire is clean and no dirt is on it.

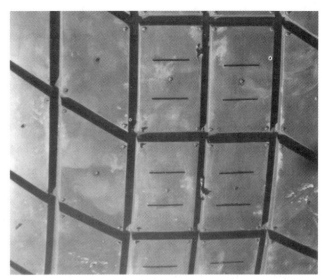

Sipe cuts allow heat to build in the tire quickly and lets a harder tire start working earlier.

someone will accidentally pick it up, or will burn whatever you lay it on.

Siping is done by turning the square cutting blades around backwards on a conventional groover, and letting just the sharp edge protrude through. Sipes are very thin cuts which are used to make a tread surface more pliable, to help prevent tire glazing, or to help dissipate heat out of tread blocks. Siping, when used with different conditions and patterns, lets the tire adhere to the track surface better and dissipates heat at a faster rate.

Before starting the grooving, make sure the tire is clean and no dirt is on it. Dirt dulls the blade and makes grooving difficult. You also need to spread talc powder across the area you are about to groove. This makes the blade slide easier across the tread pattern. Also, make sure the grooving iron is fully heated if you use a conventional grooving iron, or the heat range is set high enough on the deluxe model. If the heat range is not set properly, the groover tends

to tear and stretch the rubber instead of cutting a good clean cut.

Different Types of Grooves & Sipes

Grooving the tire's tread blocks puts more flexibility in them. This improves traction. The more traction that is required on a particular dirt surface, the more that a tire is grooved. Different types of grooving can tailor the tire to the track's surface. Here are some examples of different types of grooves and sipes to use on a tire for different track conditions:

Wet, tacky track early in the race program with loose dirt

Groove a lot of cross pattern grooves 1.5 to 2 inches apart. The grooves should be .25-inch wide. This will help clean away loose dirt and let the edges of the grooves dig in for maximum traction.

Tacky firm track that has packed down and is not loose

Use less cross grooves than with

the loose tacky track pattern. Cut them 2 to 3 inches apart and make the grooves 3/16inch wide.

A hard track that doesn't build heat in the tires

Use 3/16 to 1/4-inch wide grooves placed 1 to 1.5 inches apart with double cross pattern sipes.

Hard abrasive asphalt type track

Many times this type of track requires the use of circle groove tires with no side grooving. If the tire tread needs more flexibility to gain better traction, add some sipes in the tread about 3 inches to 6 inches apart.

Hard abrasive track that builds extreme heat

Some types of track surfaces will increase tire heat, even to the point of blistering the tires. Grooving can be used to release built-up heat in the tire, cooling it down and preventing blistering. Grooves will divide larger tire tread blocks into smaller blocks

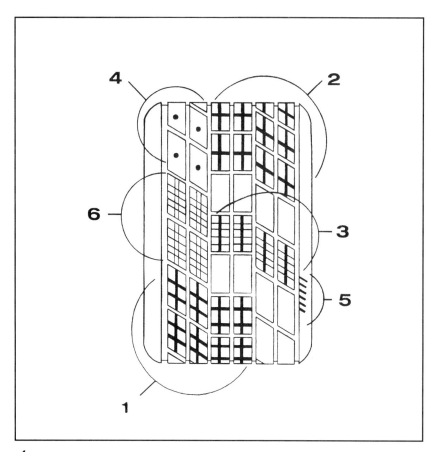

1 Vertical grooves and cross grooves are used on wet tacky tracks. They help to clean away loose dirt and let the edges of the blocks dig in for maximum traction.

2 On a tacky firm track that is packed down and not loose, use less grooving. One vertical and one cross cut in each block should be 3/16-inch wide.

3 On a hard track that doesn't build heat in the tires, use one 3/16-inch vertical groove with double cross pattern sipes. The sipes add traction and help build heat in the tires.

4 On a hard abrasive track surface, tires wear fast and heat builds up quickly. Don't modify the tread blocks other than by adding a small hole in the middle of each block to let heat escape. The hole is 3/16-inch OD, drilled to 75 percent of the tread depth.

5 Grooving the sidewall on the outside helps a tire break up loose dirt on a track surface, and works well on a track with a cushion.

6 Use one vertical sipe cut and two cross sipe cuts for a track that is getting dry and slick, but does not have a shiny surface.

which produces more air circulation and heat radiation around the blocks.

The hard abrasive track surface also wears tires fast so in order to help the tire last, a minimal amount of grooving is used. You might just groove in the center of a block instead of going all the way across. Abrasive or rough tracks can easily tear the tread blocks on a tire when they heat up, so care has to be taken not to modify the tread blocks too much. We use a drill bit that drills a small hole in each block which lets heat escape and yet maintains maximum strength at the same time. A 3/16-inch drill bit is modified with a stop on it so the bit will not penetrate too deeply. The proper depth is 75 percent of the tread depth.

Other Grooving Tips

All of the grooving we have talked about here uses basic square-shaped grooves. V-shaped grooves work well on tracks where you need grooving for traction early, but as the tire wears, the groove gets smaller and more tire is on the ground for maximum traction. A V-groove would be used for a track that gets more hooked up and abrasive as the night goes on.

Another way to lengthen tire life is to not groove as deeply into a tire. In the early stage of a race, the grooves are available to help traction. As the tire wears, the grooves decrease and eventually disappear. This type of grooving is ideal for a track surface that requires a lot of tire surface in the late stages of a race.

Grooving the sidewall helps a tire break up loose dirt on a track surface, and works well on a track

GRT sells this handy tire grooving and grinding station. It features adjustments up to 180 degrees with five position stops, free turning or lock-in positions in 30-degree increments, and interchangeable wheel bolt pattern.

If you don't have time to run some laps on new tires, use a sander on them to scuff the shiny surface off.

with a cushion. Run the groover straight across the shoulder edge of the tire at the same angle as the inside blocks. Be careful not to cut too far around the edge so that the sidewall is not damaged. The grooving depth would start out the same as on the tread face, but taper down to nothing as the shoulder edge is approached.

Proper Angles for Grooving

Grooving tires at angles instead of straight across depends on whether the car will be driven sideways more than straight on a race track. The back end of a race car will always be operating at some angle, depending on track conditions. A very heavy wet track will see the rear of the car hanging out a lot more than on a very slick, asphalt type of track.

The grooves which are cut into the tires must be placed at an angle which is consistent with the operating angle of the car. If a tire

grooved for a dry slick asphalt type of track, the grooves will be at much less of an angle than those which are cut for a heavy, wet track surface.

The reason for angled grooving is to keep the grooves perpendicular to the direction of travel. This allows the grooves to do their most efficient work on the track surface.

Front Tire Grooving Tips

Front tires perform better with a circumferential groove. Since these tires steer the car, a lot of cross grooving is not necessary. The grooves around the circumference of the tire put some flexibility in the tread blocks, and this helps increase traction. The edges of the circumference grooves will bite into the track as the car is steered, improving the steering response.

Tire Break-In

Breaking in or scuffing tires is important for prolonging tire life and improving their traction capability. We believe that running a few laps on a tire and getting that smooth edge off of the tire will help the tire gain traction quicker. In 100 lap events, tires have to be properly cured to prevent blistering and wear. We run tires in hot laps and build heat in them, then we immediately dowse them with cold water. This cures the tires and helps them last longer in a long race.

If you don't have time to run some laps on new tires, another way to scuff tires is to use a sander on them. We use an air sander and lightly run an 80 grit disc over the surface area of the tire to knock off the shiny film. We believe that scuffing a tire will be an advantage to your starts.

Tire Pressure

Tire air pressure on most late

This tire is a little too soft for track conditions. The rubber is tearing off.

This is a good wear pattern for a tire. The tire was run brand new – it was not cured with a heat cycle. That is why the edges of the blocks are feathered.

model dirt tires is very close on all applications, regardless of the type of tire used. I have talked to a lot of different race teams and most everyone will be within 1 or 2 pounds of pressure in each tire at most race tracks.

This is what works best under almost any track condition:

LF 8 to 9 PSI	**RF 10 to 11 PSI**
LR 5 to 6 PSI	**RR 9 to 10 PSI**

These air pressures should be checked before each race, and before each chassis setup. Accurate stagger cannot be checked without correct air pressure, so this is very important.

When setting air pressure, make sure that the tire is properly seated all the way around the wheel. We inflate each tire to 25 PSI to make sure it is seated properly, and then let the air back down to the desired pressure.

These suggested air pressures will keep a tire bead properly seated under race conditions. The only wheel that requires a bead lock is the right rear. This may be hard to believe, but we only use a bead lock on right rear tires.

You can use bead locks on all four corners if you desire, but it is not necessary.

However, if a track is extremely rough and there is a cushion, then you may need bead locks on both right side tires. Mud plugs (plastic insert hub caps) may also be used to prevent mud from building up in the rim which would cause a severe shake from being out of balance.

Reading Tire Surfaces

You can tell a lot by how a tire surface looks. This will help you determine if the compound is correct and the grooving and siping patterns are correct.

If the rubber on the surface is peeling back and ripping away, you probably have too soft of a tire. If the tire has just started working on the edges and they look like they are going to start peeling back soon, then the compound is close, but should probably be a little harder with some grooving and siping added.

If the surface of a tire is glassy or shiny smooth, then the compound is too hard. If that is the case, and you are limited to using this particular tire compound, then start experimenting with grooving and siping. When you get to the point that the rubber is actually tearing or chunks are coming out of the tread, too much grooving and siping has been used.

For the optimum tread surface appearance, you are looking for a surface that kind of "grains over" and resembles a sandpaper type of surface. The rubber is working and forming to the track surface, but it is just hard enough to keep from tearing or peeling.

If the tire starts blistering or "bubbling," then you must try to get rid of some heat and start thinking about saving your tires with chassis setup and driving style. This is the only option you have when you are running as hard of a tire as you can get and it still blisters and bubbles.

Tire Stagger

Tire stagger is dependent on the track conditions and the way the car is set up to work. We usually set our front tires up with .5-inch to 1-inch of stagger. This stays the same for almost all track conditions.

Rear tires are much more critical. Stagger plays a big role in the handling of a race car, and you will have to learn when and where to use the proper amount of stagger. GRT cars like a lot of stagger in the rear. We use 4 to 7 inches of stagger at most tracks. Our cars are tight and they need the stagger to help the car turn and go through the apex of the corner. This is really critical when the track has any bite to it or when a track gets hooked up.

A lot of this has to do with driving style as well. When you reduce the stagger, it will tighten the car. If the car already is tight, then the driver will have to compensate to make the car turn. This in turn causes the car to break loose or tail out. This is what you don't want. Using less stagger makes this problem worse. So unless the car is extremely free and you can drive a car with less stagger, the corner speeds are usually slower.

The rear stagger that we recommend for GRT cars is:

7"	**Wet heavy track**
6"	**Tacky, good traction**
5"	**Average track, high speed or momentum track**
4"	**Dry slick track**

There are race tracks which we run that sometimes require us to use 3 to 4 inches of stagger, but not often. Other cars might

Tire stagger generally ranges between 4 and 7 inches. A tacky track with good traction requires 6 to 7 inches of stagger.

require less stagger. However, as a general rule, if the stagger is in the 4 to 6-inch range, you will be in the ballpark. Experiment with 1 to 2 more inches of stagger, and see how the chassis reacts with it on different track conditions. Keep good records of the stagger used at each track, and always check it before the car is scaled.

Wheels

This is a subject that every racer talks about, including which style, what offset, what kind, bead locks or no bead locks. The first decision is what kind of wheel to run. Mostly this depends on the class rules for your application.

Aluminum Wheels

Aluminum wheels are the most common wheel used in late model dirt racing. We have used several different brands and sell two or three. We currently use the Weld wheel.

Aluminum wheels are light and durable. They absorb crash dam-

age well and keep on racing unless it is a severe accident. One word of caution when shopping for aluminum wheels is to always make sure that you know what you are getting. Aluminum wheel manufacturers offer different thicknesses of material in their wheels, and some are truer than others. The thinner wheels are going to be the lightest and will cushion an impact better. So make sure to get all of the specifications on the wheels before buying.

Aluminum wheels come in a variety of widths, offsets and bolt patterns. In the wide 5 style wheel, the Weld XL series wheel has multiple bolt pattern holes that are used as lightening holes. This also assists in faster tire changes by not having to line up only one set of bolt holes.

Aluminum wheels also have a variety of bead lock styles and mud cap combinations. The current wheel we use has a ring that fits in between the bead lock ring and the wheel edge that has Dzus springs installed. This system lets a

The Weld XL series wide 5 style wheel has multiple bolt pattern holes that are used as lightening holes. This also assists in faster tire changes.

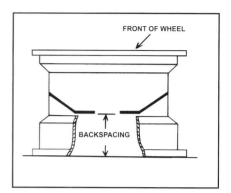

Wheel backspacing is the distance from the back face of the wheel to the back of the hub-mounting center of the wheel. To measure backspacing, lay the wheel with the back side down on the shop floor. Measure from the floor to the back side of the center section of the wheel.

crew member install or remove the mud cover quickly. It is very durable and reliable when running against some of the most severe cushions and muddy conditions that are sometimes encountered.

Wheel Trueness

Wheel trueness is probably more important than any other part of the wheel's rotating performance (other than weight). All newly purchased wheels should be checked for lateral and radial run-out. Lateral run-out is the sideways movement, commonly referred to as wobble. Radial run-out is the true roundness of the wheel.

We check our wheels once or twice a year for trueness. What we do is bolt the wheel securely to a hub mounted on the car and rotate the wheel using a dial indi-

cator mounted on a jack stand or something equivalent. When the wheel rotates, take a reading from the wheel edge. We have seen wheels with as little as .030-inch run-out, and some with as much as .070-inch. The ones closer to .030-inch are the choice wheels. Each Winter when racing season is over, check your wheels. Replace or repair any wheels that are out more than when they were new.

Wheel Offsets

Wheel offsets commonly are available between 2 inches and 7 inches. At GRT, we have designed our cars using a 5-inch offset wheel. This makes life much easier for the racer and crew. You don't have to wonder about which tire goes on which wheel because of different offsets. All the wheels

can be the same.

Obviously different offsets are required to tune a chassis for different conditions. To accomplish this, we use a wheel spacer to change the offset of our wheels. This really simplifies the process and does the same thing as installing a different offset wheel, provided the spacer is the same width as the offset you are changing. You can put a 2-inch wheel spacer on and bolt up a 5-inch offset wheel and have accomplished the same thing as using a 3-inch offset wheel. If you use a 1-inch spacer, you would have a 4-inch offset wheel. This is much easier than changing tires around on wheels.

No matter what kind of car you race, try to standardize the wheel offset. It will save you money and a lot of time.

When experimenting with offsets, make sure that the back spacing does not interfere with any suspension or brake parts on the car. Sometimes a back space that is too deep will cause a tire to rub or a wheel to hit a steering rod end, a shock or a spring mount. Make sure you check all clearances.

Also, changing offsets on wheels changes weight distribution, and changes the scrub radius on front steering. Take all of this into consideration when determining the offset of the wheels you choose.

Valve Stems

Most all of the wheel manufacturers install valve stems in their wheels at the factory. We suggest using the chrome shoulder type valve stem with a metal screw-on top. This top goes over the entire valve stem down to its base. This protects the valve stem from minor impacts or sharp objects hitting the stem. The cap has a small rubber gasket inside it that seals against the top of the valve stem. If air leaks past the valve stem core, this cap and seal will usually prevent the air from escaping.

To check for valve stem leaks, after the tire pressures have been set, we put a little soapy water on the top of each valve stem with a spray bottle. If there is a leak, it will blow out the soapy water.

This practice ensures you don't have a leak in the valve stem areas.

Always keep extra valve stems and valve stem cores handy somewhere in your tool box in case you should experience damage to one.

Bead Locks

Bead locks are a life saver. They will hold the tire on the rim with low air pressure, and also serve as a mounting point for a mud cap. Bead locks can be used on any type of wheel. As long as the rules allow it, they should always be used on the right rear, and sometimes on the right front.

When mounting a tire, tighten the bead lock evenly and make sure the tire doesn't jump out of the beaded area. The tire has moved if the bead lock ring will not tighten evenly. When mounting bead locks we always use a 3/8-inch drive impact wrench set at 25 to 30 foot/pounds of torque. After you have tightened them with the impact, check the torque with a hand wrench for insurance.

Wheel Maintenance

Wheel maintenance is important. Wheels that are bent or cracked need to be repaired or replaced. You need to check each wheel closely three or four times a season to ensure there are no problems starting to occur. And, always check the car's wheels thoroughly for damage if you have been involved in a wreck — even a minor wheel bumping incident.

Always rotate your wheel supply and get rid of wheels that need replacing. If you keep using a bad wheel, sooner or later it will fail and could cause a crash. This tears up your equipment, and someone could get hurt.

Things to inspect a wheel for are lug hole wear, cracks or bends, trueness of the wheel, and worn or bent wheel edges.

If you have bead locks, make sure you occasionally lubricate the bead lock bolts and check the flat washers to make sure they are not rounded out. Replace any bead lock rings that are bent or cracked.

Only professionally trained persons should mount tires. Before inflation, the entire assembly of any multi-piece rim must be placed in a restraining device. Stand away from the assembly when inflating. Never exceed 25 PSI when seating a tire.

Chapter

8

Chassis Setup & Alignment

Before we set up the chassis, we have to make sure that there is no binding in the suspension, and that the rear end is set square in the car. If any of these problems are present in the chassis, they will negate any of the settings we try to make on the car.

Checking For Chassis Binds

Before doing the chassis setup in the shop, you must look for the presence of any chassis binds in your completed car. Move each of the wheels through at least two inches more than their normal wheel travel. Carefully observe the movement of everything attached to that wheel. Look for shock absorber binding or bottoming out, A-arms moving freely or contacting the frame, the steering shaft moving freely without contacting anything when turned, a free movement of all steering components through full range of left-to-right steering with no binding or contacting, the Panhard bar moving freely with no binds or without contacting any chassis parts, the torque arm moving smoothly with no contact or bind, and the rear suspension arms moving freely with no binds.

If you observe any problems, be

sure to correct them right away before proceeding to the chassis setup.

Squaring The Rear End

The rear end squaring process makes sure the rear end housing is set straight in the car — perpendicular to the vehicle centerline and not angled. If the right rear is set behind the left rear, the car will be loose. If the right rear is set ahead of the left rear, it will push.

Squaring the rear end is very critical to the car's handling. Even a 0.25-inch out-of-square can have a significant effect on handling. Even though the rear end may be trailed on the right side later on, we always start with the rear end square in the chassis so we have a baseline reference point.

Most professionally manufactured chassis have built-in squaring reference marks on the frame rails. These reference marks are

On GRT cars, the four-link brackets are square in the chassis. To square the rear end in the chassis, use the links coming back from the 4-bar brackets. Set the links at the specified length. If the link lengths are equal on each side, the rear end housing will be square in the car.

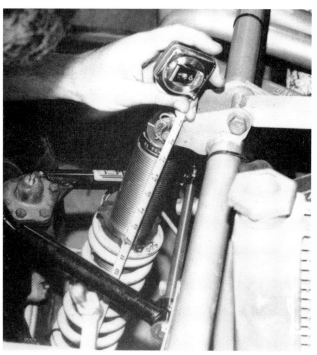

A quick and positive way to set the ride height is to measure from the top of the lower A-arm to the bottom of the main frame.

On cars that have underslung frame rails, you can use ride height blocks between the rear end tube and underslung frame rail to set the proper ride height distance between these two points.

usually holes drilled in the frame rail, or marks punched in the rails.

Make sure you know where these are.

On our cars, the four-link brackets are square in the chassis. To square the rear end in the chassis, the easiest thing to do is to use the links coming back from the 4-bar brackets. Set the links at the specified length. If the link lengths are equal on each side, the rear end housing will be square in the car.

Chassis Set-Up In The Shop

Your goal in setting up the chassis at the shop is to have the car ready to race competitively as soon as it rolls off the trailer at the track. With the car set up properly at the shop, you should have to make a very minimum amount of adjustments at the track.

Be sure that you choose a flat, level surface in your shop on which to do the setup. Always use the same place. Make marks on the floor where the car sets so it can be returned to the same location time after time.

The chassis setup should follow a specific order each time. Make sure the correct springs and shocks are in the car, and that it is completely race-ready. All fluids (fuel, oil, water, power steering fluid, transmission fluid, etc.) should be full, and the wheels and tires (including tire stagger) and air pressure should be the same as you plan to use at the track. Have the car prepared just like you are going to race it. We have the car fueled with 15 gallons of fuel because this is the median point between the start of the race and the end of the race.

Setting The Ride Height

The first step in chassis set up is to establish the recommended ride heights and front end alignment. Start with setting the ride heights at the manufacturer's recommended heights. We provide ride heights and a complete set up sheet with each car we sell.

A quick and positive way to set the ride height is to use a set distance between two reference points. We measure from the top of the lower A-arm to the bottom of the main frame. Our cars require this distance to be 3.0 inches on both the left and right front. Some manufacturers might require you to maintain a certain upper A-arm angle, but we find it is easier to use the reference distance measurement. Adjust the spring seats on the coil-overs to obtain the required measurement. Be sure to bounce the car up and down thoroughly to settle the suspension and the coil-overs. Double check the reference measurements one more time after you do this.

Once you have adjusted the two front ride heights, go to the rear. The right rear ride height is measured between the top of the lower underslung frame and the bottom of the rear end tube. 4 ¼ inches is

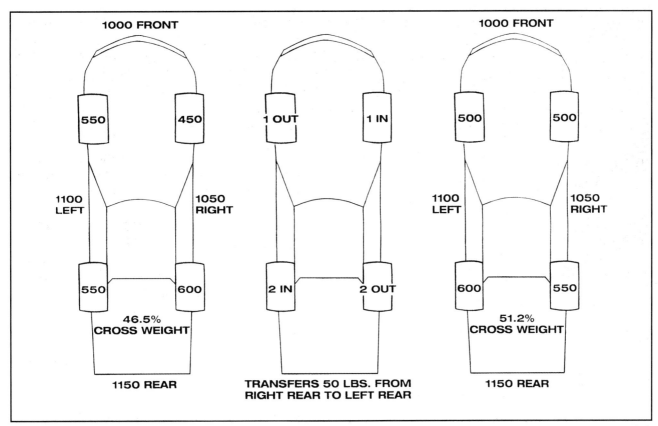

This weight jacking method transfers 50 pounds of weight from the right rear to the left rear without changing chassis ride heights. Notice what happens to the front corner weights after the change. Also notice that the total of the left side, right side, front and rear weights did not change even though the corner weights did.

our standard measurement for GRT cars at the right rear. (On older model cars with an angles underslung rail, this distance is 3 inches.) An advantage with our cars having underslung frame rails is that it allows you to use ride height blocks between the rear end tubes and the lower frame rails. These blocks set the proper ride height distance between these two points.

The rear settings are a little different due to the fact that you only need to set the ride height on the right side. Let me explain. On any race car I have ever set up, you only set three corners – the two fronts and the right rear. The reason you leave the left rear out is because you have to set the

wedge with that corner. The wedge is how much left rear corner weight you have compared to the right rear corner. If you had all four ride heights set to an exact measurement or angle, there would be no way to change the wheel weights to get what you want. So, the left rear ride height is allowed to be whatever it takes (within reasonable tolerances) in order to get the corner weights of the car set correctly.

Setting The Corner Weights

Once you set the three corners and look at the three wheel scales, you can determine what adjustments have to be made for the left rear. Let's say you have 550

pounds on the left front and 450 pounds on the right front. The right rear is 600 pounds and the left rear is 550 pounds. This gives you 50 pounds of right rear weight or reverse wedge. Your ride heights might be exactly what they are supposed to be, but you want to have 50 pounds of left rear weight or bite. The goal here is to have the left rear weigh 50 pounds more than the right rear.

Now comes the part that a lot of people have a hard time understanding. If you move the weight jacks exactly opposite of each other across the front and across the rear, the ride heights will be maintained but static weight will be moved around. For example, we are starting with 550 pounds at

Making weight adjustments on the front springs of a race car will have a greater effect than making the same adjustment on the rear springs because the front springs are stiffer rate springs.

the left front, 450 pounds at the right front, 550 pounds at the left rear, and 600 pounds at the right rear, and the ride heights are correct on each front corner and on the right rear. We want to change the weight around without changing the ride heights.

First let me explain the system I use when scaling a car. Any time you want to change 50 pounds of weight around, it is a simple system to use. Put two turns down on the left rear coil-over and turn the right rear coil-over adjuster up two turns. At the front, turn the right front coil-over adjuster down one turn. At the left front, take one turn off of the coil-over adjuster (move it up). After these adjustments to the coil-overs are made, be sure to bounce the car up and down thoroughly to settle the suspension and the coil-overs, then reweigh the car.

With these moves, you have transferred 50 pounds of weight

from the right rear to the left rear. Now you will have 550 pounds on the right rear and 600 pounds on the left rear. And most importantly, the existing ride heights will have stayed the same. You will also find that this system has moved 50 pounds from the left front to the right front, so that now both front corner weights are 500 pounds. (Note: This system might vary in its results slightly from one car to the next and may not come out exactly the same, but experiment with it on your chassis. This system works.)

Study these changes so you know what each adjustment does. To take weight off of a wheel, turn the weight jack or coil-over adjuster away from the spring. When you do this it also takes weight away from the diagonally opposite corner of the car. If you take weight off of the left rear, you also take weight off of the right front.

If you turn the weight jack adjuster toward the spring, you will add weight to that wheel and at the same time add weight to the diagonally opposite corner. For instance, adding weight at the left rear adds weight at the right front also.

Making weight adjustments on the front springs of a race car will have a greater effect than making the same adjustment on the rear springs. This is because the front springs are stiffer rate springs. One turn of a weight jacker on a 500#/" spring will jack more weight than one turn of a weight jacker on a 225#/" spring. This occurs because a stiffer spring offers more resistance to the movement of the weight jacker, thus the chassis raises or lowers

more quickly than it would over a softer spring.

Remember, to start this system you must first get the ride heights correct, and then scale the car to see where it is at. Once you know where you are, you can start moving static weight around.

Another consideration is that the left side weight percentage and the rear weight percentage will not change, no matter how you adjust the static weight by raising or lowering corners of the car. The left, right, front and rear corner weights will always add up to the same number regardless of what changes are made to each corner weight by adjusting corner heights. The only way to change one of these percentages is to add or subtract weight to the car or change wheel offsets. So, for instance, if you scale your car and you have 53% left side weight and you want 54% left, you must add ballast or move components around, or change wheel offsets. We do not recommend changing the wheel offset on our cars to change a percentage, so you must add ballast to the most practical area. Make sure that when you add ballast, the weight is securely bolted to the chassis by a ballast clamp or to a welded insert in the frame.

Ballast Placement

The height of the ballast in the chassis has an effect on the handling of a car more so than just what the scales say. For instance, having 54 percent left side weight that uses 75 pounds of weight mounted low in the chassis will react differently than 75 pounds that is mounted high. So always take this into consideration when

The adjustable motor plate makes up and down engine adjustments easy for changing overturning moment. The standard position is in the lowest engine position. But if a racer knows he will be going to a track that is consistently dry slick, he can raise the mounting position of the engine up to help produce more right side tire grip.

The anticipated track surface condition at the end of the race will influence how the weight percentages are set for the chassis. A track that is antici-pated to stay "hooked up" will require more left side weight percentage. However, if the track will be dry slick at the end of the race, more rear weight percentage (more rear ballast) would be required.

mounting ballast.

Ballast location should be con-sidered for all track conditions. With drier smoother or slicker tracks, place the ballast higher in the chassis. For rough, hooked up tracks, the ballast should be placed lower in the chassis. The higher that weight is placed in the chassis, the more overturning moment there will be during cor-nering. The overturning moment promotes side bite or right side traction during cornering. Heavy or hooked-up tracks create a lot of side bite for the tires, so the car does not need additional over-turning moment. However, dry slick tracks create very little side bite, so more overturning moment is required for right side traction.

So, ballast is placed higher in the chassis on these tracks to create the desired effect.

Once ballast is added to the chassis, the car most likely will settle and ride heights will have to be adjusted accordingly. We also recommend that the caster and camber be set before final scale readings are made.

Setting Up For The End Of The Race

The most common way to set a car up for the final scale reading is to have the chassis set up with the fuel load the way that it will be at the finish of a race. The reason is that the minimum weight you can have is when the race is over. So, you want to have the chassis scaled based on the optimum per-centages with the car at its mini-mum weight.

When a car is set up to be neu-tral handling at the end of the race with a nearly empty fuel load, that

means the car will start a race with an understeering condition when the fuel cell is full. The driver may need to use brake bias adjust-ments to help the handling until the car starts to neutralize. The car will get looser as the fuel burns off, so a compromise has to be made for the setup at the beginning of the race. You don't want the car to be loose at the end of the race.

The anticipated track surface condition at the end of the race will influence how the weight per-centages are set for the chassis. A track that is anticipated to stay "hooked up" (good moisture and traction) will require more left side weight percentage. However, if the track will be dry slick at the end of the race, more rear weight percentage (more rear ballast) would be required.

Don't get the chassis too light. Remember to use enough ballast in the chassis to get it to minimum weight with a very low fuel load.

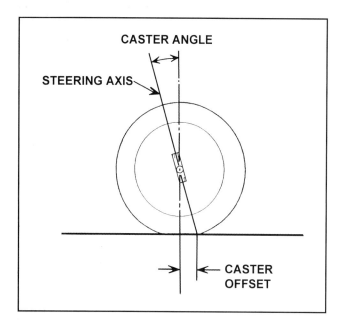

Give yourself some room here so you don't get disqualified for being too light after a race.

Front End Alignment

The front end alignment is the process of setting the desired camber and caster at each front wheel, plus setting the toeout.

Camber is the inward or outward tilt of the wheel in the vertical plane. Negative camber tilts the top of the wheel inward toward the centerline of the car. Positive camber tilts it outward away from the centerline of the car.

Caster is viewed from the side of the wheel. Positive caster places the top ball joint behind the center of the lower ball joint. Negative caster is the opposite. Negative caster is rarely used in stock car chassis settings.

Camber, caster, and toe-out are very important settings for the proper handling of a race car and should be checked often. These affect tire wear and steering stability. Incorrect toe-out will cause a darting condition. Check these settings before each race. Most probably if the camber, caster, or toe-out is not correct after you have properly set them, you have a bent ball joint or some other suspension component which is bent or broken.

Caster

Setting the caster should be done before the camber because camber is affected by caster.

Caster provides directional steering stability. This influence is created with a line which is projected from the steering pivot axis down to the ground. This line strikes the ground in front of the tire contact patch when the caster is set in the positive position. A torque arm then exists between the projected steering axis pivot line and the center of the tire contact patch. The torque arm serves to force the wheel in a straight ahead direction. The greater the length of this torque arm (caused by greater amounts of positive caster), the greater the steering effort required to turn the wheels away from their straight ahead direction.

The difference in caster setting between the left front and right front is called caster stagger. A slight amount of caster stagger helps the car change from its straight ahead path more easily to ease into a left turn. This caster stagger is created by having the caster at the right front greater than the caster at the left front.

The caster stagger on a dirt track car is generally not very large because the same factor which aids in turning the car to the left increases steering effort when turning to the right to countersteer. Most drivers are generally comfortable with a 2-degree caster split between the left front and right front on dirt.

Positive caster jacks wedge into a chassis. When a particular wheel with positive caster is steered, it raises the spindle height, and thus jacks weight to the diagonal rear corner. The greater the positive caster, the more weight that is transferred. Positive caster increase cross weight when the front wheels are turned to the right as the driver counter steers.

The amount of caster and caster stagger used on a race car is also influenced by the use of power steering. Cars with power steering can use more positive caster and more caster stagger.

Setting The Caster

On most dirt late models, caster is set by adjusting the lower strut rod back and forth. If you pull the lower A-arm forward with the strut rod, you add caster to the wheel. If you push the wheel back by lengthening the strut rod, you take caster out. Do not adjust the caster with upper A-arms that have a solid shaft in them by using spacers that are not equal. This procedure will cause the cross shaft in the upper A-arm to be in a bind.

Use the following caster settings:

LF: +1.5°   RF: +3°

GRT's No Sweep Caster/Camber Gauge

GRT sells a caster/camber gauge which reads caster directly without the need to rotate the wheels 20 degrees in each direction.

This gauge works by precisely machining a square keyway into the end of a spindle snout. There is a spindle keyway cutting kit available to work with the gauge. Once this keyway is cut, a key stock on the gauge is mounted into the keyway on the spindle and caster is read directly.

The gauge reads caster and camber simultaneously, displaying camber from 0 to 6 degrees and caster from 0 to 8 degrees.

Camber

The purpose of the camber adjustment is to keep the tire contact patch flat on the track surface at the maximum point of cornering. Camber has the biggest influence over the vehicle's cornering ability than any other alignment feature. On most dirt late model cars, the static camber setting at the right front tire is between 3 and 4 degrees negative, depending on the camber change curve of the suspension, the type of track and banking, the tire construction, and the tire tread width. In general, wider tires use less initial camber, and narrower tires use more.

Spacing the upper A-arms in or out adjusts camber in or out. Moving the upper A-arm in toward the vehicle centerline adds

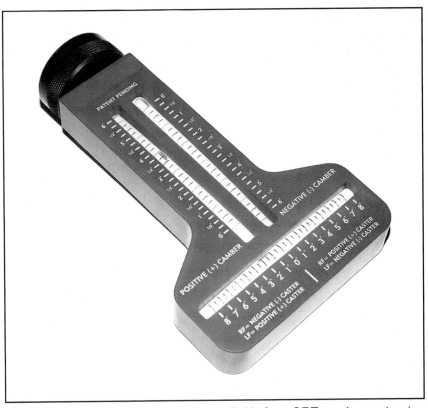

The no sweep caster/camber gauge available from GRT requires no turning of the front wheels back and forth to obtain a caster reading. It reads caster and camber simultaneously. You can also use it to measure caster and camber curves.

negative camber. Moving it out adds positive camber.

Use the following guidelines for the initial camber settings (track testing may show that initial settings may need to be changed):

LF: +1° to +2°   RF: –3° to –4°

Tire temperatures taken after practice laps will help you determine the exact camber requirements for your application.

Setting The Toe-Out

We recommend use ¼-inch toe-out on short tracks, and ½-inch toe-out on faster and longer tracks. This amount of toe-out serves to stabilize the race car, preventing weaving and wandering. This

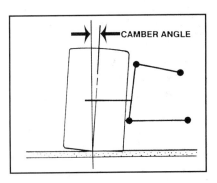

range of toe-out is a little higher than many others recommend, but we have done back-to-back and found that the additional toe-out produces no noticeable drag. What you have to realize is that when you set toe-out, you are measuring it at spindle height. But you don't see the same amount of toe-out at the tire contact patch. It is less at the contact patch.

Toe-out is set by measuring the difference between the front of the tires and the rear of the tires at spindle centerline. There are several ways to accomplish this, but one of the easiest is to use a trammel bar set solidly against the right front tire. The other end of the bar has a pointer set a few inches away from the left front sidewall. Measure from the pointer on the bar to the sidewall at the same height front and rear on the tire.

When measuring to the sidewalls to find and set toe-out, you have to be very careful about sidewall distortions. Tires can have high and low variations that can easily make your measurements off by at least 1/4-inch. So before measuring for the toe-out, run through this procedure first to assure you have valid reference points:

Jack the wheel up and rotate the tire against a fixed reference point, such as a jack stand. In doing this you are looking for the highest and lowest spot on the sidewall. Mark the highest and lowest spots with chalk, and then put those marks at the top and bottom when you are doing your measurements for toe-out. Every time you make an adjustment on the toe, you have to roll the car back and forth before you re-measure. With the chalk marks at the top and bottom, you know you are getting the same reading every time.

Once an adjustment has been made, roll the car back and forth to take up any slack in the linkage. If the car had to be jacked up to make the change, also bounce the car up and down before taking a new toe measurement.

When setting the toe-out for a

If you are going to a track that has a cushion or is extremely rough, you need to sitffen the right side of the car.

dirt track car, split it equally between the left front and right front wheels. For example, if you are using ¼-inch toe-out, set 1/8-inch out at the left front and 1/8-inch out at the right front.

Checking the amount of toe-out is a real quick way of determining if anything in the front end has been bent due to contacting something on the track. Be sure you know what the toe-out setting was when the car went out on the track. If the car bangs wheels with another car, or hits something, be sure to check the toe-out right away. If it has changed, chances are something is bent.

Starting Specs

The following chapter offers complete setup specifications for cars racing on many different types of track configurations and conditions. Refer to these for your baseline chassis setup.

Chassis Setup & Adjustments

The setup should be done with the car race ready and with 15 gallons of fuel, but with no driver. This is a car with a 32-gallon fuel cell, and which starts a race with a full fuel load. If you start the race with a lesser fuel load, scale the car with 50 percent of the fuel load you start a race with. We usually base most settings on an average of a 180-pound driver. If the driver weighs more or less, then allow for this in your calculations. For example, if the driver weighs 225 pounds, then the left side percentage would be less because of the additional driver weight. The main thing about setting your car up is do it the same way every time and in the same place. Be consistent.

Let's say that you are going to a track that has a cushion or is extremely rough. Then you need to plan on stiffening the right side of the car. Shocks should be increased to a 76 at the right front and a 95 at the right rear. Spring rates will usually increase 50 pounds in the front and 25 pounds in the rear. You can judge a lot of this by your shock indicator travel, which is a good reference.

Shock absorber travel on the right side of the car will give you a good guideline for proper chassis performance. On our cars we look for 2.75 to 3 inches of shock compression travel on the right rear and 3.25 inches on the right front. The shock travel would be the same for a wet, muddy track, a moist hooked-up track and a dry slick track. The difference would be in the shocks and springs used in the car for these different track conditions to maintain this travel.

Extremely smooth, dry race tracks generally will require a little softer springs and shocks. And, split valve shocks could be used for better weight transfer. See the chassis tuning chapter for more details on using these shocks.

Generally front end settings don't change a lot between track conditions, but camber will be adjusted more than other settings because of the banking of the race track. A greater banking angle

Shock absorber travel on the right side of the car will give you a good guideline for proper chassis performance. Look for the same amount of travel whether the car is on a wet, muddy track, a tacky track, or a dry slick track. The difference would be in the shocks and springs used for these different track conditions.

generally requires more negative camber at the right front. Check tire temperatures and tire wear to determine required camber changes. Evaluate the differences in tire temperatures across the face of each tire, comparing the inside, center and outside edges of the tires.

Chapter
9

Track Setups

Baseline Setup

This setup is the baseline chassis settings for a flat to medium-banked 3/8-mile track, with good traction, packed dirt. All numbers are based on a 2004 GRT dirt late model chassis.

Weight Distribution [1]

Left   52.5%
Rear   55.0%
Cross   51.0%
LR bite 150 pounds

Ride Heights

Left Front
3" top of lower control arm to bottom of frame

Right Front
3" top of lower control arm to bottom of frame

Left Rear
Will be set with amount of bite

Right Rear
4 ¼" top of underslung rail to bottom of axle tube
3" older cars with angled underslung rail

Springs

LF	500	RF	350
LR	250 (behind axle)	RR	225

Front springs are 10" tall
Rear springs are 12" tall

Notes:
(1) Scale the car without driver, and with 15 gallons of fuel
(2) All shock absorber pounds of force measured at 4.7 inches per second piston speed.

Shocks (twin tube)

LF	75	RF	75
LR	99-3	RR	94

Shocks (gas pressure monotube)

LF
90# compression [2]
150# rebound
100 psi gas pressure

RF
80# compression
160# rebound
100 psi gas pressure

LR
135# compression
40# rebound
200 psi gas pressure

RR
65# compression
115# rebound
75 psi gas pressure

Torque Arm Shock
60# compression
175# rebound
100 psi

Torque Arm

Length:	36"
Fifth coil shock:	73-6
Fifth coil spring:	325 (10" tall spring)
Preload:	¼"
Sixth coil:	400#/"

Front End Alignment

Caster

LF: +1 ½°   RF: +3°

Camber

LF: +2°   RF: -3 ½°

Toe out

¼" to ½"

Rear End Lead

Right rear back ¼" to 3/8"

Stagger

5"

4-Bar Settings

Left Upper
7th hole up (23° to 25°)
17" long

Left Lower
3rd hole up (6° to 7°)
15" long

Right Upper
5th hole up (18° to 20°)
17 ½" long

Right Lower
4th hole up (level)
15 ½" long

J-Bar Settings

19 ¼" center-to-center length
Third notch up on chassis
Second notch up on pinion bracket

Banked and/or High Speed Tracks

Weight Distribution

Left   52.5%
Rear   54.0%
Cross   51.0%
LR bite 150 pounds

Ride Heights

Left Front
3" top of lower control arm to bottom of frame

Right Front
3" top of lower control arm to bottom of frame

Left Rear
Will be set with amount of bite

Right Rear
4 ¼" top of underslung rail to bottom of axle tube
3" older cars with angled underslung rail

Springs

LF	500	RF	400
LR	250 (behind axle)	RR	250

Shocks (twin tube)

LF	75	RF	76
LR	94	RR	94

If there is some traction in the track or built-in momentum, add a dummy shock in front of the left rear axle. Use real shock behind axle.

Shocks (gas pressure monotube)

LF
90# compression
150# rebound
100 psi gas pressure

RF
150# compression
190# rebound
100 psi gas pressure
Tune to track condition by increasing gas pressure

LR
135# compression
40# rebound
200 psi gas pressure

RR
65# compression
115# rebound
75 psi gas pressure

Torque Arm Shock
60# compression
175# rebound
100 psi

Torque Arm

Length:	36"
Fifth coil shock:	73-6
Fifth coil spring:	325
Preload:	¼"
Sixth coil:	400#/"

Front End Alignment

Caster

LF: +1 ½°   RF: +3°

Camber

LF: +2°   RF: -3 ½°

Toe out

¼" to ½"

Rear End Lead

Right rear back ¼" to 3/8"

Stagger

5"

4-Bar Settings

Left Upper
7th hole up (23° to 25°)
17" long

Left Lower
3rd hole up (6° to 7°)
15" long

Right Upper
5th hole up (18° to 20°)
17 ½" long

Right Lower
4th hole up (level)
15 ½" long

J-Bar Settings

24 ¼" center-to-center length
Third notch up on chassis
Second notch up on pinion bracket

Extremely Slick or Slow Track, Semi-Smooth To Smooth Tracks

Weight Distribution

Left   52.5%
Rear   56.0%
Cross   51.0%
LR bite 150 to 200 pounds

Ride Heights

Left Front
3" top of lower control arm to bottom of frame

Right Front
3" top of lower control arm to bottom of frame

Left Rear
Will be set with amount of bite

Right Rear
4 ¼" top of underslung rail to bottom of axle tube
3" older cars with angled underslung rail

Springs

LF	550	RF	325*
LR	250 (behind axle)	RR	225

*Soften right front spring in 25#/" increments to as low as 300#/"

Shocks (twin tube)

LF	75	RF	74-6
LR	99-3	RR	93

Shocks (gas pressure monotube)

LF
90# compression
150# rebound
125 psi gas pressure

RF
80# compression
160# rebound
50 psi gas pressure

LR
135# compression
40# rebound
200 psi gas pressure

RR
65# compression
115# rebound
75 psi gas pressure*
  *Reduce to 50 psi for a smooth slick track

Torque Arm Shock
60# compression
175# rebound
100 psi

Torque Arm

Length:	32"
Fifth coil shock:	73-6
Fifth coil spring:	300#/"
Preload:	¼"
Sixth coil:	400#/"

Front End Alignment

Caster

LF: +1 ½°   RF: +3°

Camber

LF: +2°   RF: -3 ½°

Toe out

¼" to ½"

Rear End Lead

Right rear back ¼" to 3/8"

Stagger

4"

4-Bar Settings

Left Upper
7th hole up (23° to 25°)
17" long

Left Lower
3rd hole up (6° to 7°)
15" long

Right Upper
5th hole up (18° to 20°)
17 ½" long

Right Lower
4th hole up (level)
15 ½" long

J-Bar Settings

19 ¼" center-to-center length
Third notch up on chassis
Second notch up on pinion bracket

Very Tacky, High Traction Tracks

Weight Distribution

Left   52.5%
Rear   55.0%
Cross   51.0%
LR bite 75 pounds (using longer lower left link)

Ride Heights

Left Front
3" top of lower control arm to bottom of frame

Right Front
3" top of lower control arm to bottom of frame

Left Rear
Will be set with amount of bite

Right Rear
4 ¼" top of underslung rail to bottom of axle tube
3" older cars with angled underslung rail

Springs

LF	500	RF	375 to 400
LR	250 (behind axle)	RR	300

Shocks (twin tube)

LF	75	RF	75
LR	94*	RR	94

*Mount in front of axle, with spring on dummy shock behind axle

Shocks (gas pressure monotube)

LF
90# compression
150# rebound
100 psi gas pressure

RF
80# compression
160# rebound
100 psi gas pressure

LR

135# compression
40# rebound
200 psi gas pressure

RR
65# compression
115# rebound
75 psi gas pressure

Torque Arm Shock
60# compression
175# rebound
100 psi

Torque Arm

Length:	36"
Fifth coil shock:	73-6
Fifth coil spring:	350
Preload:	¼"
Sixth coil:	400#/"

Front End Alignment

Caster

LF: +1 ½°   RF: +3°

Camber

LF: +2°   RF: -3 ½°

Toe out

¼" to ½"

Rear End Lead

Right rear back ¼" to 3/8"

Stagger

6" to 7"

4-Bar Settings

Left Upper
Upper hole (30°)
17" long

Left Lower
5th hole up (10°)
19" long

Right Upper
5th hole up (18° to 20°)
17 ½" long

Right Lower
4th hole up (level)
15 ½" long

Using the above longer left lower link setup, reduce the left rear bite from 150 lbs. to 75 lbs.

J-Bar Settings

24 ¼" center-to-center length
5" of rake

Chapter
10

Track Tuning & Adjustment

Dirt track racing is notorious for changing track conditions. The track will continually change its characteristics from when you first get to the track, into hot laps, heats and features. This means that the driver or crew chief will have to know when and how to make adjustments to the car to correct handling problems on a wet track, tacky track, hooked up track and dry slick track.

First you must determine what kind of track conditions you will be running on. Through the hot lap session, you can learn what the car needs. One factor that you must take into consideration is that the chassis must be set properly before you can make any other adjustments. Camber, caster, toe-out, tire pressure, tire compound, and brake bias must be set properly. If these items are not set correctly, then you will never stand a chance at setting up your car to track conditions.

Chassis Tuning Elements

There are a variety of chassis tuning elements that can be used to adjust the race car to changing track conditions or to correct handling problems. In the following sections we will define these and

discuss how each can be used to influence the handling behavior of the car. Then we will discuss various track conditions from wet and heavy to dry and slick, and how to adjust the chassis for these.

Finally, there are sections on common handling problems, with information on how to adjust the chassis to solve them.

Left Rear Shock Placement

There are three different shock placement setups used at the left rear to tune the car to track conditions. These are: a real shock and coil spring by itself mounted

behind the axle housing; the real shock (with spring) mounted behind and a dummy shock in front; and a real shock mounted in front and a dummy shock with coil over spring mounted in back.

Maximum traction and forward drive is obtained by using a real shock mounted behind the housing, with nothing in front. Use this arrangement on an extremely slick smooth track to gain maximum traction.

Adding a dummy shock in front of the axle housing at the left rear slows down the reaction at the left rear and the driving force of the left rear tire. It adds resistance to

Dirt track racing is notorious for changing track conditions. The track will continually change its characteristics from when you first get to the track, into hot laps, heats and features. The driver or crew chief will have to know when and how to make adjustments to the car to correct handling problems on a wet track, tacky track, hooked up track and dry slick track..

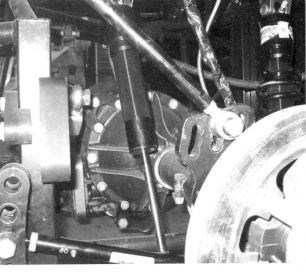

Putting the real shock on the front and a dummy shock with a coil spring behind slows down forward drive traction due to the way the birdcage indexes.

Maximum traction and forward drive is obtained by using a real shock mounted behind the housing, with nothing in front.

the suspension as the throttle is applied and shows down the indexing of the left rear birdcage. This configuration works best on tracks with traction or on momentum tracks.

Putting the real shock on the front and a dummy shock with a coil spring behind slows down forward drive traction due to the way the birdcage indexes. Having the real shock in front makes it slower to load the left rear as the throttle is applied. This type of setup works on tracks with some traction, semi-banked momentum tracks, and wet heavy tracks.

Left Side Weight Percentage

More left side weight percentage loosens a car at corner entry, and tightens it at corner exit under throttle. The more left side weight percentage a car has, the less left rear bite it needs.

Left Rear Bite

Left rear bite is defined as how much more corner weight the left rear has than the right rear. For example, if the right rear weight of a car is 550 pounds, and the left rear is 675, the car has 125 pounds of bite.

Adding more left rear bite makes a car loose at corner entry, and tighter at corner exit under acceleration.

Rear Weight Percentage

The rear weight percentage should range between 54 percent and 56 percent, depending on the track conditions and configuration. The baseline setup is 54.5 to 55 percent rear weight. The highest amount of rear weight is used on a real short stop-and-go track.

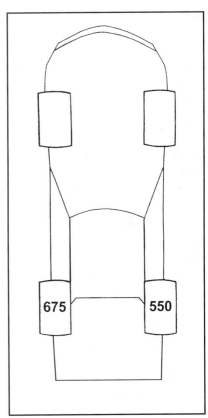

Left rear bite is defined as how much more corner weight the left rear has than the right rear. This car has 125 pounds of bite.

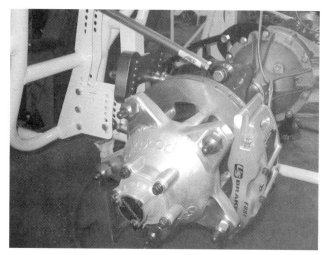

Adding more upward angle at the left upper link and decreasing the angle at the right upper will deliver more reaction force to the left rear tire. This gives the left rear more forward drive traction and tightens up the chassis.

The upper right bar is used when the track has a lot of traction. Increase its upward angle to help the car turn through the middle of the corner.

On slow speed, slick or tight cornered tracks, the rear weight can be increased up to 56 percent. Because the car has to be slowed so much for corner entry, more rear weight is required to get good forward drive under acceleration.

On a higher speed, momentum track, increasing the rear weight beyond 54 percent will loosen up the car at corner entry. Using less rear weight here keeps the back end of the car more stable at corner entry and through the middle, helping the driver be more consistent.

Rear Upper Link Adjustment

When the left and right side upper links are inclined differently, it can place different reaction forces on the left and right tires. If the right upper link is angled upward more, and the left upper link angle is reduced, more reaction force is delivered to the right rear tire under acceleration. This produces more right rear trac-

tion, which is good for a tacky track. On the other hand, adding more upward angle at the left upper and decreasing the angle at the right upper will deliver more reaction force to the left rear tire. This gives the left rear more forward drive traction and tightens up the chassis, which is desirable for a dry slick track.

When using the 4-link angles to adjust the chassis to changing track conditions, normally the left upper and right upper bars are used. The left upper angle is changed when the track has no traction. Increase the upward angle when the car needs more forward drive and more roll steer to turn through the middle of the corner.

The upper right bar is used when the track has a lot of traction. Increase its upward angle to help the car turn through the middle of the corner. When the right upper link is angled upward more than the left upper, more reaction force is delivered to the right rear

tire under acceleration. This produces more right rear traction, which is good for a tacky track. Increasing the upward angle on the right upper bar also increases roll steer, which helps the car turn on a tacky track.

Tire Stagger

Tire stagger is dependent on the track conditions and the way the car is set up to work. We usually set our front tires up with .5-inch to 1-inch of stagger. This stays the same for almost all track conditions.

Rear tires are much more critical. Stagger plays a big role in the handling of a race car, and you will have to learn when and where to use the proper amount of stagger. GRT cars like a lot of stagger in the rear. We use 4 to 7 inches of stagger at most tracks. Our cars are tight and they need the stagger to help the car turn and go through the apex of the corner. This is really critical when the track has any bite to it or when a

Move the proportioning adjustment to favor rear braking bias (about 70 to 75 percent rear) to start for a wet, heavy dirt surface. This helps to loosen the car at corner entry.

track gets hooked up.

A lot of this has to do with driving style as well. When you reduce the stagger, it will tighten the car. If the car already is tight, then the driver will have to compensate to make the car turn. This in turn causes the car to break loose or tail out. This is what you don't want. Using less stagger makes this problem worse. So unless the car is extremely free and you can drive a car with less stagger, the corner speeds are usually slower.

The rear stagger that we recommend for GRT cars is:

7"	Wet heavy track
6"	Tacky, good traction
5"	Average track, high speed or momentum track
4"	Dry slick track

Brake Bias

Brake bias is the proportioning of the total braking force between the front wheels and rear wheels. Moving the brake bias to favor the front wheels makes a car tend toward understeer under braking

at corner entry. Moving the brake bias to favor the rear wheels makes a car tend toward oversteer under braking.

Move the proportioning adjustment to favor rear braking bias (about 70 to 75 percent rear) to start for a wet, heavy dirt surface. This helps to loosen the car at corner entry. As the track dries out, continue to move the adjustor to favor the front brakes. For a dry slick track, you may find it necessary to use 65 to 70 percent front bias. Too much rear brake on a dry slick track is going to get the car loose at corner entry.

Chassis Tuning With Ballast Placement

Dirt track cars require weight to transfer onto the right side tires during cornering in order to make the right side tires bite and hold the car. This is true in all cases except on a tacky high traction surface. If it didn't do this, the right side tire contact patches would slide outward. In order to achieve this side bite effect, the weight has

to be properly positioned in the chassis.

Weight that is located above the roll axis of the car will more easily transfer during cornering and be planted downward on the right side tires. The higher that weight is located, the more it will be accelerated in an arcing motion to the right side during cornering by a moment arm about the roll axis. This means the weight transfer is leveraged by the moment arm (the distance between the center of gravity height and the roll axis). Conversely, weight that is located below the roll axis will transfer straight across, pushing laterally on the tires and creating a lateral shear force at the tire contact patches.

Moving the ballast mounting location in the chassis can help to adjust for track conditions. When the track provides good traction, mount the ballast low and to the left. Mount it on door bars, in front of the driver's seat or on the left frame rail. Keep the weight centered (front to rear) in the chassis.

On a real slick track, raise the ballast higher in the chassis and to the right to provide more roll and weight transfer to the right. This provides more downward weight transfer onto the right side tires to get them to stick

If the car is pushing at corner entry on a dry slick track, mount some ballast weight at the right front corner. Typically 15 to 25 pounds of ballast is mounted on the chassis tubes above the right front tire. This will help the tire to grip the track and help the car to turn at corner entry.

On momentum type tracks, if the car is tight at corner entry, move the ballast weight forward

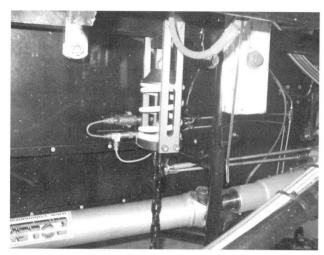

Weight that is located above the roll axis of the car will more easily transfer during cornering and be planted downward on the right side tires.

If the car is pushing at corner entry on a dry slick track, mount some ballast weight at the right front corner. Typically 15 to 25 pounds of ballast is mounted on the chassis tubes above the right front tire.

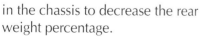

A movable battery box allows for adjusting weight transfer and/or percentages. The battery is dead weight that can easily be used for a handling advantage as long as it is movable.

The Panhard bar is attached to a pinion mount on the rear end housing. This forms a pivot point for the sprung weight of the chassis as the body rolls during cornering. The angle between the chassis mount of the bar and the pinion mount of the bar influences how the chassis rolls about the pivot point.

in the chassis to decrease the rear weight percentage.

On a stop-and-go type of track, move the ballast weight rearward in the chassis to increase rear weight percentage.

Tuning With the Panhard Bar

The Panhard bar is attached to a pinion mount on the rear end housing. This forms a pivot point for the sprung weight of the chassis as the body rolls during cornering. The angle between the chassis mount of the bar and the pinion mount of the bar influences how the chassis rolls about the pivot point.

The Panhard bar angle is extremely important in achieving body roll and left rear forward drive. More angle (between the

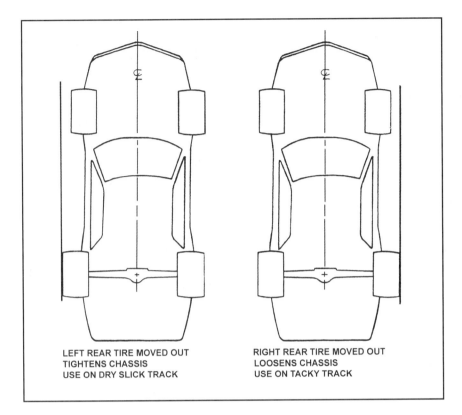

LEFT REAR TIRE MOVED OUT
TIGHTENS CHASSIS
USE ON DRY SLICK TRACK

RIGHT REAR TIRE MOVED OUT
LOOSENS CHASSIS
USE ON TACKY TRACK

chassis mount and the pinion mount) accelerates the process. More angle gets a car up on the bars quicker.

The standard baseline Panhard bar setup uses 7 ½ inches of rake. That means the center of the pinion mount is 7 ½ inches lower than the center of the chassis mount of the bar. This number can go up to as much as 9 inches, and as low as 5 inches.

The higher amount of angle (going toward 9 inches of rake) is used for flat, slick and slow tracks where side bite and forward drive are hard to get. If the car needs more roll up and forward drive, use more Panhard bar angle. If there is a lot of traction in the track, it requires less bar angle or rake.

A flatter bar angle (going toward 5 inches of rake) is used for tacky, higher speed, and good traction tracks. The flatter angle takes away some of the body roll.

Tuning With Wheel Offset/Wheel Spacers

Using a wheel spacer or changing wheel offset makes the car loose or tight, depending on where the change is made. Going from a 5-inch offset right rear wheel to a 3-inch offset wheel (moving the tire out away from the body) will free the car up or make it turn by doing two things:

First, it will place more static weight load on the left rear. Usually a 2-inch offset change will move about 22 to 25 pounds to the opposite side of the car when you move the wheel out. This frees the car at turn entry.

Second, with the wheel being further out on the right rear, it will take away side bite and not pin

the right rear tire as hard so the car is free all the way around the corner. This helps the car turn easier on a tacky hooked up track.

The opposite occurs when you space the left rear wheel out away from the car. That tightens the car at turn entry and helps create side bite all the way around the corner. The reason this happens is because spacing the left rear out loads the right rear corner. This tightens the chassis at corner entry, which pins the right rear harder and creates side bite. Using more wheel offset at the right rear and less at the left rear would be a desirable chassis adjustment for a dry slick track.

Wheel spacers are used sometimes for a quick fix. Using a wheel spacer is easier than using wheels with different backspacing.

Use a wheel spacer at the right rear when the track is tacky. This will loosen the car. Use a wheel spacer at the left rear to tighten the car.

Tuning With Shock Absorbers

Shock absorbers control the rate of weight transfer during cornering, they control spring movement, and they control suspension movement over bumps and surface undulations. Being able to control the chassis with the proper shock absorbers is a key element to proper handling on dirt. Shocks can be used to help control handling problems or to induce desirable handling characteristics.

Shocks have no effect on the amount of weight that is transferred dynamically during braking, acceleration and cornering. They can, however, affect the transient response in the pitch and roll axis. The amount of weight transferred is dependent on the center of gravity, roll axis, and roll rates. How quickly the weight is transferred is controlled by the shock absorbers.

Track speed and the amount of traction available are important elements for choosing the proper shock absorber. For example, the slicker or slower a track is, the softer the shock absorber you should use. The faster or heavier a track is, the stiffer the shock should be. Shock absorbers have to be changed on the car as track conditions change. This keeps the suspension tuned to the track.

If you are in doubt about the choice between two different shock rates, choose the softer one. In almost all cases, softer shocks will yield faster lap times. Softer shocks generally make a car faster because they let weight transfer quicker to a wheel. This puts the transferred weight to work quicker and plants that corner of the car for maximum traction.

Refer to the shock tuning chart at the end of this chapter for specific recommendations.

Tuning With Split Valving Shocks

There are conditions when you want to use a shock that has a different valving in compression than in rebound movement. For example, you may want to keep a particular corner of a car from transferring a lot of weight when it rises up, which would require a stiff rebound valving shock, but you don't want to have a stiff shock for compression or bump travel at that corner. In that case, a split valving shock can be used. A split

Shock absorbers control the rate of weight transfer during cornering, they control spring movement, and they control suspension movement over bumps and surface undulations. Being able to control the chassis with the proper shock absorbers is a key element to proper handling on dirt. Shocks can be used to help control handling problems or to induce desirable handling characteristics.

On a dry slick track, a 3-5 (3 compression, 5 rebound) tie down shock is used at the right front to create and hold side bite. The softer 3 compression valving helps a car to roll over onto the right front. The stiffer rebound valving helps to maintain side bite.

valving shock has one rate in compression, and another rate in rebound.

Tie down shocks have stiffer valving in rebound than compression. That means the shock compresses more easily than it pulls apart.

On a dry slick track, a 3-5 (3 compression, 5 rebound) tie down

Front-to-rear brake proportioning is critical. Use pressure gauges front and rear to initially set the brake balance. Using pressure gauges also helps to spot a master cylinder that is going bad.

shock is used at the right front to create and hold side bite. The softer 3 compression valving helps a car to roll over onto the right front. The stiffer rebound valving helps to maintain side bite and does not let the car get back on the left rear too quickly, especially under acceleration. At that point the car is getting more bar angle at the left rear and forward drive, so keeping the car rolled over on the right front as long as possible helps the car turn and reduces a push condition.

At the left rear, an "easy up" shock is used. This is a shock which is very soft in rebound and very stiff on compression. The left rear shock is generally a 9-3 (9 compression, 3 rebound). The stiff compression is designed to keep the left rear corner up on the bars, and to allow a slow transition when the driver gets off the throttle and the left rear falls down. This makes the chassis less reactive for the driver because the 4-

bar angles and roll steer change as the left rear corner falls. The soft 3 rebound allows the left rear corner to get up on the bars quickly.

Chassis Tuning With Gear Ratio

Gear ratio is also a factor in tuning a chassis. Our theory on gear ratio is to gear a car as if you could use every single horsepower developed by the engine, and your car was hooked to the max. Remember that the track does not change in size, just condition. Using a slightly lower gear ratio enables the driver to be smoother because he won't bog the engine. If the track becomes hard and slick, the driver can gradually ease into the throttle. The gear should help slow the car down on corner entry and therefore braking won't be as extreme. This in turn makes a more consistent and smoother driver, which creates faster lap times.

On a dry slick track, the gear

ratio may need to be changed, depending on where the driver wants to run on the track. If he wants to stay on the very bottom, a lower ratio would be used. If he feels that he can be faster by running at the top of the track, a slightly higher gear ratio would be used.

Different Types Of Track Conditions

Through an evening of racing at a typical dirt track, a racer will see several different types of track conditions. Generally, a track will start out very wet. The dirt may be very heavy, if the water is worked down into the track, or it may be very slippery if the water is just setting on the very top of a harder dirt surface. Under these conditions, it is very difficult to make a car turn left. The rear wheels are providing forward traction while the front wheels want to skate forward as they are turned.

Once the water is packed down into the track, it produces a tacky track condition. This is a type of surface where the tires can really bite into the dirt and gain good traction — good side bite and good forward bite.

Finally, as the water evaporates out of the dirt and the dirt packs down, it gets very hard and slick. When the track gets that way, the back end of the car gets very loose and it is difficult to get any forward traction.

Let's discuss some of the different types of track conditions and different handling problems associated with these conditions.

Wet Track Condition

The first thing you must do when the car goes out on the track is make sure the brakes are working properly. This is one of the areas that affect the handling of a race car on any track condition, so double check this every time. The car has a balance bar on the brake pedal assembly and you should make sure that it is working properly. Then make sure you know which way to turn the balance adjuster crank to gain more front brake or more rear brake.

A good rule that many racers go by for balance bar adjustment is: turning the adjuster clockwise puts front brake into the car. Turning it counter clockwise puts rear brake into the car. This makes the adjustment easy to remember. Make sure you know what your brakes are doing when you turn the adjuster crankb.

Most probably your car will have an understeer or push condition on a wet track. When we are talking about a wet track, we mean one that has not yet been packed down all the way and still has a lot of water on the surface. This type of condition usually won't stay long and therefore you probably won't be racing long on this kind of track. Normally this type of track has been rained on by the water truck and takes a little while for it to be packed in. There are adjustments that can be made to help cure problems in this area, but don't overdo it because the track won't stay this way long.

With a push condition on a wet track, the first thing to check is the brake balance. For this type of track, it should be adjusted for about 75% rear brake bias. This will make the car set or tail the

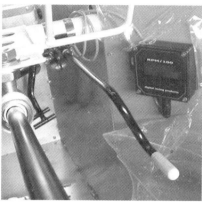

A good rule for balance bar adjustment is that turning the adjuster crank clockwise puts front brake into the car. Turning it counterclockwise puts rear brake in the car.

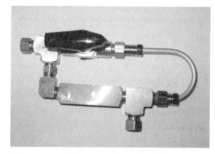

On a wet, heavy track, it is very easy to lock up the right front wheel, so use a brake shut-off valve to control this. This shut-off valve has a pressure relief valve installed. Many times fluid will leak past the shut-off valve which will cause the right front caliper to push the pistons out and lock the pads against the rotor. The pressure relief valve prevents this.

On a wet track there is limited traction and you are basically sliding around. The chassis setup needs to force the tires to dig into the track surface, so you need to create side bite and forward bite.

rear out when you are entering the corner. This is the most important factor to get a car to enter the corner properly on a wet track.

This works just the opposite if a car has a loose condition or oversteer on wet dirt. If the problem is oversteer, put some brake bias

back into the front.

On a wet, heavy track, it is very easy to lock up the right front wheel, so a brake shut-off valve is used to control this. If the car enters the corner and pushes, make sure the valve is set to shut off pressure to the right front

Tacky tracks usually cause a car to push because the rear tires grip the track so well. The most important adjustment for a tacky track condition is to free the car up. The chassis has to be loosened up to decrease right rear side bite.

brake. In addition to preventing right front wheel lock up, this also creates a pulling effect to the left when the brakes are applied. This will help the car set up for a corner on a wet track.

Once the car has entered the corner and you have the car set properly, the next step is to make sure it gets around the corner. This sometimes is as difficult as anything on a wet track because there is limited traction and you are basically sliding around. The chassis setup needs to force the tires to dig into the track surface, so you need to create side bite and forward bite.

Use as soft a tire as possible, and one that is grooved well for this type of condition. Use plenty of tire stagger in the rear — in the range of 5 to 6 inches. Don't use a lot of left side weight because this usually creates a push condition on a wet track. Move ballast to the right.

Lower the Panhard bar height in order to create more roll and right rear side bite. The ballast should be mounted high in the chassis.

Using a shorter length torque arm (adjusting it to a shorter distance from the rear end to lift point) will usually assist in this type of condition. A torque arm that is too long sometimes will lift the car's front wheels (or lighten up the front end) and create a push condition.

Remember that any adjustment used to correct a push condition described here, the opposite type of adjustment usually corrects a loose condition for a race car.

The Tacky Track

The wet track condition usually changes quickly to a tacky track, and it usually lasts longer than the extremely wet track. Therefore you should take this type of condition more seriously than a wet track because you will be running

on it longer.

Tacky tracks usually cause a car to push. This is because the rear tires grip the track so well. The most important adjustment for a tacky track condition is to free the car up. The chassis has to be loosened up to decrease right rear side bite.

A tacky race track usually starts sometime during time trials or early in the heat races and usually fades to a dry or rubbered down race track by feature time. So qualifying in time trials or heat races is very critical. This requires a good set up for a tacky track. Most of the time a tacky race track provides a lot of traction. You want a race car that will turn and be extremely fast through the corners due to the traction that will be available in the track. On a tacky track, side bite or body roll is not nearly as critical as it is on a dry track.

There are a number of ways the chassis can be adjusted for this condition:

1) Set the Panhard bar higher in the chassis than normal, and close to level. This raises the rear roll center which keeps the car looser. Less angle in the bar keeps the right rear from planting down hard which causes a push condition in the middle of the corner.

2) At the left rear, mount the real shock in front of the axle tube, and a dummy shock with the coil over spring on it behind the axle. This slows down the loading at the left rear as the throttle is applied. The tackier the race track, the more you have to slow down the action of the suspension at the left rear.

3) Use more rear brake bias than normal on a tacky track to get the car to set, but not as much as used

A stiffer right rear spring helps free a car up under acceleration on a tacky track. Stiffer right front and right rear shock valving prevents weight transfer from occurring too quickly.

A tacky track requires a lot of stagger – in the 5 to 7-inch range. The tire compound should be the softest available because a tacky track requires maximum front and rear bite.

on a real wet track. Brake pressure to the right front brake should still be shut off.

4) A stiffer right rear spring helps free a car up under acceleration on this type of track. Increase the right rear spring rate by 25#/" to 50#/". A stiffer right rear spring will make a car tighter at corner entry when the driver is off the throttle.

5) A stiffer right rear and right front shock valving helps on a tacky track. These shocks stabilize the car and prevent weight transfer from occurring too quickly. Change from a 75 to a 76 at the right front, and from a 94 to a 95 at the right rear. These are easy changes if you are using adjustable shocks.

6) Ballast placement is another chassis tuning tool. Placing the ballast lower on the left side frees the car and helps it turn on a tacky track.

7) A tacky track will let you take full advantage of a 4-link rear suspension. Creating more rear roll steer and/or increasing the right side wheelbase will help the car turn on tacky tracks. Move the right upper link all the way up. This increases roll steer and helps the car turn. Move the left upper link down one hole to reduce forward drive. Don't move it any more because that will take away roll steer.

8) Keep the torque arm length set at the shortest adjustment (usually 32 inches) to prevent the front end from pushing. The torque arm spring rate can also be increased. The baseline fifth coil spring rate is 325#/". For a tacky, high traction surface, use a 350#/" spring rate.

9) A tacky track requires a lot of stagger – in the 5 to 7-inch range. The tire compound should still be the softest available because a tacky track requires maximum front and rear bite.

10) Increase left side weight percentage to 53 ½ percent (baseline is 52 ½ percent). This will loosen the car at corner entry and up to mid-corner.

11) If the car is tight at corner entry to mid-corner, use a wheel spacer at the right rear to loosen the car.

Not all of these adjustments are necessary for a tacky track. Make the easiest adjustments first and see how your car responds. Then if more help is required in a cer-

Dry track conditions usually require softer springs and shocks, higher ballast placement in the chassis, and less left side weight percentage. Lowering the Panhard bar will help create side bite and roll on a dry track because it lowers the rear roll center.

If a car is loose on turn entry and through the middle of a turn on a dry slick track, stiffen the left front spring rate or add right rear weight.

tain area, try some of the other adjustments listed above.

Dry Track Conditions

Dry track conditions usually require softer springs and shocks, higher ballast placement in the chassis to induce roll, and less left side weight percentage. Lowering the Panhard bar will help create side bite and roll on a dry track because it lowers the rear roll center.

Dry tracks usually require a somewhat harder tire compound. Tire compound is definitely an important chassis tuning tool. Always lean toward a harder tire compound if there is any doubt.

Some general chassis tuning guidelines for dry, slick tracks are as follows:

1) If a car is loose on turn entry and through the middle of a turn, stiffen the left front spring rate, or add right rear weight.

2) If a car is tight on turn entry, soften the right front spring to add side bite, or add left rear weight.

3) If a car has four wheel drift in a corner, it has too much low left side weight. Create more side bite by moving the left side ballast higher in the chassis.

4) Lower the rear roll center by lowering the Panhard bar mounting height.

5) Add more angle to the Panhard bar to increase rear wheel loading.

6) Stagger should be decreased on a dry track. If you used 5 to 7 inches of stagger on a tacky track, decrease it to the 4 to 5-inch range for a dry track.

7) The right front brake should be operational.

8) The torque arm length should be set at 34 to 36 inches.

9) Use a softer fifth coil spring rate. Use a 300#/" spring (baseline spring rate is 325#/").

10) Use the 4-link angles to create harder and quicker forward drive. Refer to the section on this earlier in this chapter, and also in the Rear Suspension chapter.

Adjustments for Common Handling Problems

The following sections discuss common handling problems the racer is going to encounter, with information on how to adjust the

Adding more angle to the Panhard bar increases rear wheel loading and tightens up a car on a dry slick surface. This is a very radical angle for the Panhard bar.

Use the 4-link angles to create harder and quicker forward drive on a dry slick track.

chassis to solve these problems.

Hiking Up the Left Front Corner

One problem with a dirt late model 4-bar setup is that the suspension can get adjusted to the point that the car severely picks up the left front corner of the car under acceleration. The 4-bar suspension system is designed to lift the left side of the car, but it is not supposed to carry the left front corner. The left front tire should maintain traction with the track surface.

If a car is hiking up the left front, there are three areas for adjustment that help the problem: Panhard bar angle, right front spring rate, and 4-bar angles on the left rear.

With the Panhard bar, take some angle out of the chassis-to-pinion mounting points. The bar angle is extremely important in achieving body roll and left rear forward drive traction. More angle accelerates the process and gets the car up on the bars quicker. Using a flatter angle will take away some

If a car is hiking up the left front, there are three areas for adjustment that help the problem: Panhard bar angle, right front spring rate, and 4-bar angles on the left rear.

of the body roll and help keep the left front down.

Using a straight Panhard bar accelerates this problem even more. If a car is severely hiking up the left front corner, use a J-bar (with a reduced angle) rather than a straight Panhard bar.

Using a stiffer right front spring will also help to limit body roll and keep the car flatter at the front.

The 4-bar angles on the left side also have a major influence on how the car lifts on the left side. Taking some angle out of the left upper bar will help to decrease lift on the left front.

Loose at Corner Entry

If a car is loose at corner entry, one way to fix this is to increase the left front spring rate. This will

If a car is loose at corner entry, one way to fix this is to increase the left front spring rate. This will tighten up the chassis at corner entry. Under throttle application, a stiffer left front spring will load the right rear harder.

On a heavy or very tacky track, use a 94 shock at the left rear. Mount the shock in front of the rear axle housing, and mount the coil spring on a dummy shock behind the axle. This takes away from the hard instantaneous forward drive under acceleration.

tighten up the chassis at corner entry. If you have a 500#/" spring at the left front, and the car is loose at corner entry, change it to a 550#/" spring. Changing the left front spring rate will have an effect on chassis behavior at corner exit. Under throttle application, a stiffer left front spring will load the right rear harder.

Instead of changing the spring rate at the left front, you can stiffen the compression valving of the left front shock. This has the same effect as using a stiffer spring, but it will not affect the right rear corner at exit.

Another way to tighten up the chassis is to lower the height of the Panhard bar, which lowers the rear roll center height. Lower the bar equally at both ends. The lower roll center height increases side bite at the right rear tire. This adjustment will keep the car tighter through all three phases of cornering.

When a car is loose at corner entry and the driver is off the throttle, change the right rear spring to a stiffer rate. If the left rear spring is stiffer than the right rear, the car will pivot and turn about the left rear because it has more traction. Using a stiffer right rear spring rate makes a car tighter at corner entry because it takes away the left rear traction advantage. With a stiffer right rear spring, the car will be looser under throttle application at corner exit.

Reducing rear brake bias will make the car tighter at corner entry when the driver is on the brakes.

Pushing At Corner Entry/Mid Corner

When the car is pushing at corner entry or mid corner, the goal is to stick the right front tire to the track so it does not skate across the track surface. Part of that process is using a softer right front spring rate. It helps to accelerate weight transfer to the right front. It adds side bite to the right front for increased track grip.

Raising the center of gravity higher helps overturning mass to create side bite. This is done by placing ballast up higher in the car. A higher CGH helps create more body roll, and a softer right front spring helps to place that weight downward on the right front tire contact patch to make it grip the surface.

Pushing At Corner Entry

If a car is pushing or tight at corner entry, one way to loosen the chassis is to use a softer rate spring at the left front.

Another option is to use more left rear bite or wedge. This will loosen the car at corner entry, but it will make the car tighter at corner exit.

Adding left side weight percentage will also loosen the car at corner entry, but it will make the car tighter at corner exit.

Adding more rear brake bias will make the car looser at corner entry when the driver is on the brakes.

Chassis Adjustment – Wet, Heavy Track

On a wet, heavy or very tacky track, use a 94 shock at the left rear. Mount the 94 shock in front of the rear axle housing, and mount the coil spring on a dummy shock behind the axle. This takes away from the instantaneous forward drive under acceleration, and keeps the rear of the car freer so it turns good through mid-corner and corner exit.

Once the track starts to get slick, change the left rear shock to a 99-3 mounted behind the axle tube.

Also, on a wet, heavy to very tacky track, take angle out of the Panhard bar. Normal rake (the difference in mounting height between the chassis mount and the pinion mount) on the Panhard bar is 7 ½ inches. Take this down to 5 inches on a wet heavy track by lowering the chassis mount side and raising the pinion mount side. The flatter angle takes away

When a track is slick and smooth, use a 3 valving shock at the right rear. The softer valving shock accelerates body roll for faster weight transfer to the right rear.

On a track that is rubbered down or an asphalt condition, mount the left rear coil-over in front of the housing tube because the car does not need the extra traction provided by mounting the coil-over behind.

some of the body roll and added rear wheel traction.

Chassis Adjustment With Shocks – Slick Smooth Track

When a track is slick and smooth, use a 3 valving shock at the right rear. The softer valving shock accelerates body roll for faster weight transfer to the right rear. This helps gain side bite and forward traction.

If a monotube shock is being used, and it is difficult to get side bite, reduce gas pressure by 25 PSI.

High Speed/High Banked Track Adjustment

On a high banked or high speed

track, mount the left rear coil-over behind the axle, and use a dummy shock in front of the axle. Using a dummy shock in front helps to slow down the initial transfer to the left rear and takes away some of the immediate forward drive traction at the left rear.

Chassis Adjustment – Tight At Entry Under Braking

If a car is too tight at corner entry under braking, change the sixth coil spring to a stiffer spring rate. If a 400#/" spring is installed, change it to a 600#/". The stiffer spring rate will cause a more sudden braking torque reaction in the chassis, which will loosen the chassis.

If the car is still too tight at entry under braking, take the sixth coil unit off and replace it with a limiter chain.

Chassis Adjustment – Rubbered Down Track

Mounting the left rear spring behind the axle housing provides maximum forward traction. But there are situations where the spring is mounted in front.

On a track that is rubbered down or an asphalt condition, mount the left rear coil-over in front of the housing tube because the car does not need the extra traction provided by mounting the

coil-over behind. This type of track condition already provides maximum traction.

Chassis Sorting Philosophy

When sorting out handling problems with your car, make sure you are honest with yourself on what the car is doing. Make sure you know where the chassis baseline is at — don't guess. Have all of your chassis settings written down.

If you think the car is loose, really think about if you are having to make the car break loose to make it turn. I've often seen it where a driver has to make his car turn and creates his own loose situation. Yet he didn't realize why his car was actually loose. The real problem is that the car was tending toward understeer going into the corners. Make sure that you are adjusting the chassis for the correct problem.

And remember that all chassis tuning will be in vane unless tire stagger, tire pressure, front end alignment, tire compound, springs, and ride heights are correct. Before any track tuning or adjusting can be done you must have these properly set.

One thing that we have noticed through many years of racing is that a race car which tends toward being loose is faster under all track

conditions. When a car is too tight and pushes, the driver cannot be smooth and consistent. Any time a driver is smooth, he is faster. If a driver learns to drive a car in a loose condition, he can adjust to different track conditions much easier.

What you have to realize when driving a race car is that just because a car feels faster to you does not mean that it is faster. Time and time again I have seen lap times be so much quicker when the driver makes smooth consistent laps. Keep the car under you and let the car roll through the corners. Remember that once you get a car hung out with oversteer, you are losing time.

With the different set of handling dynamics that dirt late model cars present, and their naturally tight handling, a driver has to be more aggressive in lots of track conditions. Smoothness is still a factor, but more so on slower and slicker tracks. Tackier tracks and tracks with more traction need to be approached with more aggression to make cars turn because they are so tight. But they still will turn because of roll steer and horsepower. Then as tracks get slicker, the smoothness factor becomes more important.

Chassis Adjustment Quick Reference

Loose At Corner Entry

1. Decrease rear brake bias
2. Decrease angle of right lower link
3. Lower rear roll center
4. Use 3 valving shock at right rear
5. Increase left front shock compression valving
6. Increase left front spring rate
7. Move ballast higher and to the right
8. Increase angle of right upper link
9. Decrease bite
10. Stiffen right rear spring

Loose At Mid-Corner

1. Decrease stagger
2. Lower rear roll center
3. Use 3 valving shock at right rear
4. Move ballast higher and to the right

Loose At Corner Exit

1. Decrease stagger
2. Increase angle of left upper link
3. Decrease angle of right upper link
4. Increase left rear bite
5. Increase Panhard bar angle
6. Shorten torque arm length
7. Mount left rear spring behind axle without a dummy shock in front
8. Soften right rear spring

Loose At All 3 Phases of Corner

1. Decrease rear weight percentage
2. Move ballast higher and to the right
3. Lower rear roll center

Tight At Corner Entry

1. Increase rear brake bias
2. Decrease right front spring rate
3. Move ballast lower and to the left
4. Increase left rear bite
5. Increase left side weight percentage
6. Use a 73-5 shock at right front
7. Decrease angle of right lower link
8. Stiffen 6th coil spring
9. Soften right rear spring rate

Tight At Mid-Corner

1. Decrease right front spring rate
2. Move ballast lower and to the left
3. Decrease rear weight percentage
4. Increase rear stagger
5. Increase angle of right upper link

Tight At Corner Exit

1. Add dummy shock in front of axle at left rear
2. Lower left upper link
3. Raise right upper link
4. Increase stagger
5. Decrease rear weight percentage
6. Use longer lower left rear link
7. Take bite out of left rear
8. Stiffen right rear spring

Tight At All 3 Phases of Corner

1. Decrease rear weight percentage
2. Increase left side weight percentage
3. Increase stagger

Tuning With Shocks
(With left rear shock behind axle)

Loose At Corner Entry
1. Increase RF compression
2. Decrease RR compression
3. Increase rebound on 5th coil shock

Loose In Middle – Off the Throttle
1. Increase RF compression
2. Decrease RR compression
3. Increase rebound on 5th coil shock

Loose In Middle – On the Throttle
1. Decrease RR rebound
2. Increase gas pressure in LR shock
3. Decrease RR compression
4. Decrease RF rebound

Loose At Corner Exit
1. Decrease LR rebound
2. Increase gas pressure in LR shock
3. Decrease RR compression

Push At Corner Entry
1. Decrease RF compression
2. Increase LR compression (if LR is slamming down)
3. Increase gas pressure in LR shock (if LR is slamming down)
4. Increase RR compression
5. Decrease rebound on 5th coil shock

Push In Middle – Off The Throttle
1. Decrease RF compression
2. Increase LR compression (if LR is slamming down)
3. Increase gas pressure in LR shock (if LR is slamming down)
4. Decrease rebound on 5th coil shock

Push In Middle – On The Throttle
1. Increase RF rebound
2. Increase LR rebound
3. Decrease gas pressure in LR shock
4. Decrease LF rebound

Push At Corner Exit
1. Increase LR rebound
2. Decrease gas pressure in LR shock
3. Decrease LF rebound

Chapter
11
Suppliers Directory

ACPT
(Advanced Composite Products & Technology Inc.)
15602 Chemical Lane
Huntington Beach, CA 92649
(714) 895-5544, Fax (714) 895-7766
www.acpt.com
Carbon fiber driveshafts

AFCO Racing Products
(American Fabricating Co.)
977 Hyrock Blvd, P.O. Box 548
Boonville, IN 47601
(812) 897-0900, Fax (812) 897-1757
www.afcoracing.com
Coil springs, brake calipers and rotors, shock absorbers, all types of suspension components

Appleton Rack & Pinion
110 Industrial Drive, Bldg. E
Minooka, IL 60447
(815) 467-1175, Fax (815) 467-1179
www.apprack.com
Power rack and pinion steering systems, suspension components

ATL Racing Fuel Cells
Spear Rd. Industrial Park
Ramsey, NJ 07446
(201) 825-1400, Fax (201) 825-1962
www.atlfuelcells.com
Racing fuel cells

Russell Baker Racing Engines
505 Henley
Miami, OK 74354
(918) 540-2800
Racing engines

Bert Transmission
395, St-Regis North
St-Constant, PQ J5A2E7
Canada
(450) 638-2960, Fax (450) 638-4098
Racing transmissions

Brinn, Inc.
1615 Tech Dr.
Bay City, MI 48706
(989) 686-8920, Fax (989) 686-6520
www.brinninc.com

Racing transmissions

ButlerBuilt Motorsports Equipment
70 Pitts School Rd. NW
Concord, NC 28027
(704) 784-1027, Fax (704) 784-1024
www.butlerbuilt.net
Seats and dry sump tanks

Coleman Machine
N-1597 US 41
Menominee, MI 49858
(800) 221-1851
(906) 863-7883, Fax (906)863-2665
www.colemanracing.com
Driveshafts, brake components, suspension components

Custom Craft, Inc.
718 Taft Lane
Midland, AR 72945
479-639-2742, Fax 479-639-2628
Headers

D&M Performance Mfg.
P.O. Box 696
Dumas, TX 79029
www.dmperform.com
(800) 233-0571
(806) 935-2448, Fax (806) 935-2998
Racing seats

Dynatech Headers
975 Hyrock Blvd.
Boonville, IN 47601
(800) 848-5850
(812) 897-3600, Fax (812) 897-6264
www.dynatechheaders.com

Earl's Performance Products
189 W. Victoria St.
Long Beach, CA 90805
(310) 609-1602, Fax (310)762-6719
www.earlsplumbing.com
High performance hoses and fittings

Fluidyne High Performance
174 Gasoline Lane
Mooresville, NC 28117
704-662-8119, 888-FLUIDYNE

Fax 704-662-8120
www.fluidyne.com
Radiators and oil coolers

Frankland Racing Supply, Inc.

105 Industrial Drive West
Glade Mill Industrial Park
Valencia, PA 16059
(724) 898-2111, Fax (724) 898-3022
www.franklandracing.com
Quick change rear ends

Fuel Safe Fuel Cells

Aircraft Rubber Mfg.
250 SE Timber Ave.
Redmond, OR 97756
(541) 923-6005, FAX (541)923-6015
www.fuelsafe.com
Fuel cells

G-Force Racing Gear

1020 Sun Valley Dr.
Roswell, GA 30076
(770) 998-8855, Fax (770) 993-4417
www.gforce.com
Racing safety equipment

Goodridge

155 Rolling Hill Rd.
Mooresville, NC 28117
(704) 662-9095, Fax (704) 662-9094
www.goodridge.net
High performance plumbing

GRT Race Cars Inc.

83 S. Broadview St.
Greenbrier, AR 72058
(501) 679-2311 Fax (800) 880-0478
www.teamgrt.com
Dirt late model chassis builder, race car components

Hawk Performance

920 Lake Road
Medina, OH 44256
(800) 542-0972 Fax (330) 722-5500
www.hawkperformance.com
Brake pads

Hoosier Tire South

1919 Airbase Rd.
Louisville, TN 37777
(865) 970-3110, Fax (865) 984-0155
www.hoosiertire.com
Hoosier racing tires

Howe Racing Enterprises

3195 Lyle Rd

Beaverton, MI 48612
(998) 435-7080, Fax (888) 484-3946
www.howeracing.com
Suspension components

HPC / High Performance Coatings

14788 S. Heritagecrest Way
Bluffdale, UT 84065
801-501-8303, Fax 801-501-8315
www.hpcoatings.com
Coatings for headers and mufflers

Integra Shocks

3011 Mill Iron Rd.
Muskegon, MI 49444
(231) 773-4886, Fax (800) 441-6875
Monotube shock absorbers

Jaz Products, Inc.

1212 E. Santa Paula St.
Santa Paula, CA 93060
805-525-8800, Fax 805-525-8808
www.jazproducts.com
Seats, safety equipment, storage containers

JET-HOT Coatings

55 E. Front St.
Bridgeport, PA 19405
(800) 432-3379, (610) 277-5646, Fax (610) 277-0135
Specialty metal coatings

Kilsby Roberts Co.

5207 Scott Hamilton Dr.
Little Rock, AR 72209
(501) 568-4371, Fax (501) 568-7869
Structural tubing

KRC Power Steering

2115 Barrett Park Dr. NW
Kennesaw, GA 30144
770-422-5135, Fax 770-422-1680
www.krcpower.com
Power steering pumps

KSE Racing Products

P.O. Box 821
White House, TN 37188
(615) 672-5117, Fax (615) 672-2366
www.kse-racing.com
Power steering pumps

Mittler Bros. Machine Tool

P O Box 110
Foristell, MO 63348
(800) 467-2464, (636) 463-2464 Fax (636) 463-2874
www.mittlerbros.com

Metal fabrication equipment

Outlaw Disc Brakes
1465 Ventura Dr.
Cumming, GA 30040
(770) 844-1777, Fax (770) 844-1333
www.outlawdiscbrakes.com
Disc brakes

Oval Craft, Inc.
3579 Lake Katherine Rd.
Tunnel Hill, GA 30755
(706) 673-2942, Fax (706) 673-2385
www.ovalcraft.com
Aluminum racing components

Performance Bodies
P O Box 427
Cedar Falls, IA 50613
800-722-4641
www.performancebodies.com
Race car bodies

Performance Friction Corp.
83 Carbon Metallic Hwy
Clover, SC 29710
(866) 392-9936
www.performancefriction.com
Brake pads

Peterson Aluminum
1005 Tonne Rd.
Elk Gove Village, IL 60007
800-323-1960
Prefinished aluminum panels

Peterson Fluid Systems, Inc.
7200 E. 54th Pl.
Commerce City, CO 90022
(800) 926-7867, Fax (303) 287-1860
www.petersonfluidsys.com
Dry sump oil systems

PRO Shocks
1725 Lakes Parkway
Lawrenceville, GA 30243
(770) 449-4440 Fax (770) 449-4406
www.proshocks.com
Shock absorbers, coil-overs, springs

QA1 Precision Products, Inc.
21730 Hanover Ave.
Lakeville, MN 55044
952-985-5675, Fax 952-985-5679
www.qa1.net
Spherical rod end bearings

QA1 Shocks
5412 New Peachtree Rd

Atlanta, GA 30341
(770) 451-8811 Fax (770) 451-8086
www.qa-one.com
Shock absorbers, coil-overs, springs

Quarter Master Racing Clutches
510 Telser Rd
Lake Zurich, IL 60047
(847) 540-8999 Fax (847) 540-0526
www.racingclutches.com

QuickCar Racing Products
P O Box 647
Winder, GA 30680
(770) 867-9500, Fax (770) 307-2971
www.quickcar.net
Switch and gauge panels, race car components

Racor Filters
3400 Finch Rd.
Modesto, CA 95354
209-521-7860
Oil and fuel filters

RCI
12440 Hwy 155 S.
Tyler, TX 75703
(903) 939-1908
www.rciracing.com
Safety equipment

RTC
(Racing Transmission Components)
1000 E. 7th St.
St. Paul, MN 55106
(612) 776-9781, Fax (612) 778-1166

RAM Clutches
201 Business Park Blvd.
Columbia, SC 29203
(803) 788-6034, Fax (803) 736-8649
www.ramclutches.com
Racing clutches

Royal Purple Synthetic Lubricants
One Royal Purple Lane
Porter, TX 77365
(888) 382-6300, Fax (281) 354-7600
www.royalpurple.com

Schoenfeld Headers
605 S. 40th
Van Buren, AR 72956
(479) 474-7529
www.schoenfeldheaders.com

Speedway Engineering

13040 Bradley Ave.
Sylmar, CA 91342
(818) 362-5865, Fax (818) 362-5608
www.1speedway.com
Suspension components, quick
change rear ends

Speedway Motors

300 Speedway Circle
Lincoln, NE 68502
(402) 323-3200, Fax (800) 736-FREE
www.speedwaymotors.com
They sell almost every part necessary
for building a race car.

Sweet Manufacturing, Inc.

3421 S. Burdick
Kalamazoo, MI 49001
(800) 441-8619, Fax (269) 384-2261
www.sweetmfg.biz
Rack and pinion steering, power steering

TCI Automotive

One TCI Drive
Ashland, MS 38603
(662) 224-8972, Fax (662) 224-8255
www.tciauto.com

Tilton Engineering

P.O. Box 1787
Buellton, CA 93427
(805) 688-2353, Fax (805) 688-9407
www.tiltonracing.com
Pedal assemblies, master cylinders,
brake proportioning valves, hydraulic
clutch bearings, flywheels, starters

Trick Race Products

Brockville, ON, Canada
(613) 345-RACE
Carbon fiber driveshafts, body components

Turbo Blue Racing Gasoline

2499 E. Main St.
Batesville, AR 72503
(870) 793-3510, Fax (870) 793-4262
www.tuboblue.com

TWM Racing Products, Inc.

420 Tioga High Rd.
Pineville, LA 71360
318-640-4112, Fax 318-641-6135
Suspension components

US Brake

975 Hyrock Blvd.
Booneville, IN 47601
812-897-7651
www.usbrake.com
Racing brake systems

Weld Racing

933 Mulberry Street
Kansas City, MO 64101
(816) 421-8040, Fax (816) 242-6747
www.weldracing.com
Racing wheels

Wilwood Engineering

4700 Calle Bolero
Camarillo, CA 93012
(805) 388-1188, Fax (805) 388-4938
www.wilwood.com
Brake systems, hubs

Winters Performance Products

2819 Carlisle Rd.
York, PA 17404
(717) 764-9844, Fax (717) 764-0617
www.wintersperformance.com
Quick change rear ends, hubs

Woodward Steering

P.O. Box 4479
Casper, WY 82604
(888) STEER-US (307) 472-0550
www.woodwardsteering.com
Power rack and pinion steering systems

Wrisco Industries Inc.

355 Hiatt Dr., Ste. B
Palm Beach Gardens, FL 33418
(561) 626-5700, Fax (561) 627-3574
(800) 627-2646
www.wrisco.com
Prefinished aluminum panels

X-1R Performance Lubricants

375 Fentress Blvd.
Daytona Beach, FL 32114
(800) 747-4917, Fax (386) 271-7001
www.X1R.com
High performance lubricants